Iroquois

Folk Tales

Native American
Short Stories

by Mabel Powers (Yeh sen noh wehs)
"One who carries and tells the stories."

Dedication

These stories are lovingly dedicated
to all the children who ask how and why,
who see with wonder eyes,
and who yet believe in fairies
-Mabel Powers

Original Text © 1917 by Mabel Powers
Illustrations by Unknown Native American Artists

Revised and Edited by Lorrie L. Birchall
Iroquois Folk Tales: Native American Short Stories ©2014, 2019

ISBN: 9781500882211

Table of Contents

Iroquois Fairy Stories

Acknowledgement

If the Iroquois had not welcomed me into their lodge fires, these stories the Iroquois tell their children could not have been retold. With one or two exceptions, the ideas found in the stories have come from the lips of the Indians themselves.

EDWARD CORNPLANTER (*So son do wah*—"Great Night")

WILLIAM PATTERSON (*Ga reh hwonts*—"Power has come down")

MOSES SHONGO (*Ho non da a suh*—"Keeper of the hills")

CLIFFORD SHONGO (*Ouhn yah dah goh*—"Very dark blue sky")

CHARLES DOXON (*Hoh squa sa ga dah*—"Woodsman")

DANIEL GEORGE (*Jo ha a ga dah*—"Roadscraper")

MARY PRINTUP (*Wah le sa loh*)

DAN WILLIAMS (*Oh geh rah u reh ru ha neh*—"Running Bear")

ELI HENRY

HARRIETT PEMBLETON (*Gah do rehn tah*—"Dropping Husks")

AMOS KILLBUCK (*Har wen do dyoh*—"He has forsaken early dawn")

ALFRED JIMESON (*Har neh a oh*—"Hatchet in his hands")

WILLIAM HOAG (*O no nah*—"Very cold")

ELLEN PIERCE SHONGO (*Yea wen noh aih*—"The high word")

BAPTIST THOMAS (*Sa ha whe*—"Long feather")

ALBERT CUSICK (*Sha go na qua da*—"Made them mad")

THEODORE JIMESON (*Jah o yah*)

DAVID WARRIOR (*Dwen o gwah*)

WILLETT JIMESON (*So i as ah*—"Owner of fine cornstalks")

NANCY GREYSQUIRREL (*Gah gwah tah*—"One who lifts")

EMILY TALLCHIEF (*Gi das was*—"Wind blowing through corn")

LOUISE PIERCE LOGAN (*Ga yah was*—"The quivering heaven")

THOMAS JONES (*Gah ne yehs*—"The dropping snow")

To Arthur C. Parker—*Ga wa so wa neh*—for his careful review of the stories and assistance in securing authentic Iroquois illustrations; and to the story-tellers who so kindly welcomed me to their lodges and told their stories, I am most grateful.

-Mabel Powers, 1917

Foreword

Once our fathers own these lands of New York State. Once the Iroquois were great people. Their council fires burn from Hudson on east to Lake Erie on west, from rising to setting sun. Then White man come. He ask for small seat size buffalo skin. He take larger and larger one, till Indian have but small place to sit.

Now we have little left but stories of our fathers. They, too, will soon be lost and forgotten, but a voice has come to speak for us. **Yeh sen noh wehs**—the one who tells the stories—will carry these stories of our fathers. She will help White man to understand Indian, Indian to be understood. She will have all men brothers.

Indian's heart is glad that **Yeh sen noh wehs**, our white friend, has come to us. She have good eyes. She see right. She like things Indian. She try to preserve them. Our old men and women tell her the stories told them, many, many moons ago, when little children.

Yeh sen noh wehs write down these stories so our children and our children's children may read and know them; and so other children may learn them also. Indian tell these stories to his children to make them good and brave and kind and unselfish. May they teach other children how they should do.

Again we say, Indian is glad to have someone speak for him. He is glad to have someone write down the great and beautiful thoughts in Indian's mind and heart. We have spoken. **Na ho**.

Chief of Seneca Nation,

(wolf)   (Great Darkness)
Edward Cornplanter   so son do wah

Chief of Onondagas,

Frank Logan x (Tä-dŏ-dä-hŏh) his X mark
(Turtle)

Chief of Tuscaroras,

Grant Mt Pleasant – Ho gah wih
(Wolf)

Chief of Oneidas,

Adam Thomas – Jai jo-wás (He splits the sky)

Chief of Cayugas,

David Warrior   Dwen.o.gweh
(White Heron,)

Chief of Mohawks

James w Hill   De you he Kwen
(wolf)   (we live by)

How the Stories Came to Be

Out of the moons of long ago, these stories have come. Every tribe of the Iroquois had its storyteller who wandered from wigwam to wigwam.

Seated on warm skins by the fire, the story-teller would exclaim, "**Hanio**!" This meant, "Come, gather round, and I will tell a story." Then all the children would cry, "**Heh**," and draw close to the fire. This meant that they were glad to hear the story. And as the flames leaped and chased one another along the fire trail, they would listen to these wonder stories of the Little People, of the trees and flowers, of birds, of animals, and men. When the storyteller had finished, he said, "**Na ho**." This meant, "It is the end."

When the earth was very young, the Iroquois Children first learned how everything came to be, and just why it is that things are as they are. They told these wonderful things to their children, and their children in turn told them to their children; and those children again in turn told them to theirs, that these things might not be forgotten.

Now, but few of the children know these stories that the grandmothers and old men of the tribe used to tell. The storyteller is no longer seen wandering from wigwam to wigwam.

Why I Was Called the Story-Teller

Some time ago I was asked to speak for an Indian Society. I accepted the invitation, and that night made my first Indian friends.

My new friends told me many beautiful things about the Iroquois Children. The more I learned about the Iroquois people, and things Indian, the more interested I became. After a time I began to tell the others the things I had learned.

Soon, one of the tribes, the Senecas—the tribe to which my new friends belonged—heard that I was telling their stories. They wished to honor me, so they asked me to be present at their Green-Corn Feast, and become one of them.

So when the Green-Corn moon hung my horn in the night sky, I found the trail to the Land of the Senecas. There the Senecas adopted me into the Snipe clan of their nation. I was called **Yeh sen noh wehs**—"One who carries and tells the stories."

Thus it was that I became one of them, **Yeh sen noh wehs**—the Daughter of the Senecas.

The more I learned about them and their simple stories, the more I loved them. One day, I said I would be the storyteller not only of Senecas, but of all the tribes of the Iroquois. There are six great families of this people. Each family is called a tribe or nation.

Once, the council fires of these six nations burned from the Hudson on the east, to Lake Erie on the west, and they were a great and powerful people.

It was at the time of the Berry Moon that I hit the story trail. Since then I have journeyed through all the lands of the Senecas, the Onondagas, the Cayugas, the Oneidas, the Mohawks, and the Tuscaroras.

Like the storyteller of old, I wandered from lodge to lodge of the Iroquois. "**Hanio**," I would call, and as the Indians gathered round, I would tell them one of the stories that other Indian friends had told to me.

Sometimes this would remind the Indian Children of another story, which I did not know, and they would tell it to me. It was in this way that these stories have been gathered.

There were many days when I told my stories, but none were told in return. Few members of the tribes—these usually the oldest—could remember the stories "they used to tell."

Sometimes I heard a story as I trudged along a furrow, beside a ragged Indian who was plowing with a more ragged-looking team. Or I would listen as I helped an Indian woman prepare the evening meal, pick berries, or gather nuts.

Sometimes, as I sat by a fire down in the depths of a beautiful wood, and watched the smoke of the sacred medicine rise, a medicine man would tell me a story; or an Indian woman would drop a word, as she sat at her door weaving baskets or making beadwork.

I have put these stories into a story book, that they might not be lost and forgotten; that all the Iroquois Children and their children's children might know and tell them, and that all children might learn them as well.

The American children have no fairies of their own. They must borrow their fairies from children of other nations. I thought it very sad, so I put a magic feather in my cap, and winged moccasins on my feet. Then I went on the chase for real American wonder stories, and for real American fairies.

Had there not been a feather in the magic cap I wore, I would not have found them. But the feather pointed the way to the Nature Wonder Trail, and there I caught a glimpse of the "Little People"—the only true American fairies.

-Mabel Powers (**Yeh sen noh wehs**), 1917
"One who carries and tells the stories"

The Little People

(Jo gah oh)

All children who live close to Mother Earth come to know and to see the fairies of the flowers, the woods, the rocks, and the waters.

These fairies the Iroquois call the **Jo gah oh**, or "Little People," because they are so small. The Little People can do wonderful things. Whatever they wish, they can do. They can fly through the air. They can dart under or through the water, into the earth and through the rocks as they please, for they wear invisible moccasins and travel in winged canoes.

Their wee babies are carried on the little mothers' backs—just like the Indian's papoose. The little fathers have wonderful winged bows and arrows that can shoot any distance they wish.

The Little People bring good luck to the Indians. Whatever Indian boys and girls wish for—if they wish hard enough, the **Jo gah oh** will bring to them.

It is said that there are three tribes of these Little People—those that live in the rocks beside streams and lakes, those that hover near the flowers and plants, and those that guard the dark places under the earth.

The rock Little People are very strong. They can uproot large trees and can hurl great rocks. Sometimes they dare the Indians to a test of strength with them. They also like to play ball with stones.

The Indian Children fear the Stone Throwers, as they call them. But they love the little folk that help the flowers to blossom, and the fruit and grains to grow and ripen.

They remember these Little People in their Feasts of Thanksgiving, for do the **Jo gah oh** not help the sweet waters of the maple to flow? Do they not whisper to the growing seeds and show the way to the light? Do they not guide the runners of the strawberries, turn the blossoms to the sun, and paint the berries red? They also tint the grains, and give to the corn its good taste.

A third tribe of Little People dwell under the earth. They guard the sacred white buffaloes, and keep the serpent monsters that live in the darkness below from coming to the surface to the Indian Children.

There are trails that lead out to the sunlight, but the Little People guard them close, although sometimes a great serpent will find the trail of a spring, and will follow it and poison the waters.

Often, at night, these elves of the dark come to the upper world to dance with the other Little People.

Wherever you find a tree in a deep, dark part of the wood, around which no grass will grow, there you may be sure a dance ring has been formed. There the Little People have danced till the moon dropped out of the sky.

Dance Rattle

Story-Telling Time

The old-time Indians say that long, long ago, the Little People made a law that stories must not be told in summer.

Summer is the time for work. Bees must store their honey. Squirrels must gather their nuts. Men must grow their corn. Trees and plants must leaf, and flower, and bear their fruit.

If stories were told, plants, birds, animals, and men would stop their work to listen. This would mean poor crops and hungry people. Animals would forget to grow their winter coats and lay by their winter stores. Birds would fail to start in time for the South.

The old Indians say that the story-teller who disobeys this law of **Jo gah oh** will suffer some misfortune. Winter is the time to tell the stories, for then the work of animals, plants, and men is done—and the Little People are fast asleep.

No, it is not safe to tell stories in summer. No one knows when a bird, or a bee, or a butterfly may be listening, and may tell the chief of the Little People. Should the chief of the Little People be offended, he might cause something dreadful to happen to the story-teller.

Last summer, I came very near being changed into an animal—or something worse—just for telling stories. So an old Indian said. I do not know now how I escaped. I think it must have been because I was a White Indian. This is how it happened.

It was at the time of the Harvest Moon. I spoke for one of the tribes at their council house, and I told some of these wonder stories.

All went well until the middle of the night. Then a very old Indian came to warn me of my danger. It seems that he had been at the council in the evening, and had heard the stories told, many of which he knew.

He told me he had expected to see me change into something else right then and there. He said he would not dare to tell a story. "No, no, me afraid, evil come!" he said.

Then he wanted to know if I was a real Indian. He had been told that I was a White Indian, but when he heard me tell the stories, he said he thought I was a real Indian.

When I told him that I had not a drop of Indian blood running in my veins, he looked very solemn. At last he spoke. He told the interpreter to tell me—for he spoke but a few words of English—that the Great Spirit made a snake, a snake; a fox, a fox; a muskrat, a muskrat; a raccoon, a raccoon; a bear, a bear; an Indian, an Indian; a White Indian, a White Indian. Each must be snake, fox, raccoon, bear, Indian or White Indian, as long as he lived. Each must be himself.

Then the old man asked what disease I had, that made me go around with a feather in my hair, acting like a real Indian, if I were a White Indian.

I had no answer. And I do not know to this day, what saved me from being changed into a rabbit, a katydid, or something worse, by the chief of the Little People. I know, however, that I am very glad I am telling the stories to you, in the WINTER time.

How the Iroquois Give Thanks

The Iroquois are a grateful people. The true Iroquois never rises after eating without saying, "**Niaweh,**" which means, "I am thankful." The others reply, "**Niuh**,"—"It is well."

The Iroquois never pick a flower without thinking how kind the Great Spirit has been to cause the flowers to grow. They like flowers, and no matter how poor the Indian cabin, flowers are always to be found near.

When the Iroquois pick fruit, they give thanks to the Great Spirit and they always leave some for the "little brothers of the wood."

They do not try to pick every cherry or berry, or nut or apple, for themselves. Fruits grow for the birds and animals as well as for men, and the little brothers of the wood must not be forgotten. Some of everything that grows is left for them.

The Maple Feast

During the spring and summer, the Iroquois give several thanksgiving feasts. The first is early in the spring, at maple-sugar time. As soon as the sap begins to flow, the Maple Feast is called.

Sap Bucket

15

The Indians gather about a large maple tree. A fire is lighted near, upon which one of their number sprinkles tobacco. As the smoke rises, a prayer of thanksgiving is made to the Great Spirit, for causing the sweet waters of the maple to flow. Then the maple trees are thanked for their service to men, and protection is asked for the trees during the coming year.

When "the leaf of the dogwood is the size of a squirrel's ear," it is planting time. Then an Indian maid goes into the fields and scatters a few grains of corn, asking the aid of the Great Spirit for the harvest. The Indian always plants his seed with the growing moon, so it may grow with the moon.

The Strawberry Feast

The next feast is the Strawberry Feast and Dance.

The strawberry is one of the best gifts of the Great Spirit to his children. So greatly is it prized that it is thought to grow on the Sky Road that leads to the Happy Hunting Ground. An Indian who has been very ill, near death, will say, "I almost ate strawberries."

When the strawberry ripens, the Indians are happy. They sing their praises to the Great Spirit and dance with joy. They remember the Little People who have helped to make the berries beautiful, and they have a song of praise and dance of thanks for them as well. Without the help of the Little People, the strawberries would not be so sweet and ripe.

Last Feast of Summer

At the time of the Harvest Moon comes the last feast of the summer. This thanksgiving feast lasts four days. The Indians not only give thanks for the ripening of the corn, but for every growing thing. Therefore this feast is longer than the others, since it takes some time to name all the good gifts of the Great Spirit to the Indians, and to give thanks for them all.

There is a story of the corn in which the Spirit of the Corn is a maiden, not a handsome young chief, as one of the stories claims. This Corn Maiden was one of three sisters, and was called **Ona tah**.

The three sister vegetables—the corn, the bean, and the squash—were called the **Di o he ko**, which means "those we live on," since they are the life-giving vegetables.

These sisters lived together on a hill and were very happy. But one day **Ona tah** wandered away in search of dew for her kernels.

The Evil Spirit was watching. He seized **Ona tah**, the Spirit of the Corn, and sent one of his monsters to blight her fields. The killing winds swept over the hill, and the spirits of the squash and bean fled before them.

Ona tah was held for some time a prisoner in the darkness under the earth, by the Evil Spirit. At last a sun ray found her and guided her back to her lost hilltop. There she found that her sisters had fled. She was alone.

Then **Ona tah** made a vow to the sun that she would never again leave her fields. But she sighs for her lost sisters, and mourns the blight that came upon her beautiful fields. For since the time when **Ona tah** wandered away and left her fields, the corn has not grown so tall or so beautiful as it once did.

A Firemaker and a Peacemaker

In the olden times, tribes of Indians did not always live in one place as they do now. They sometimes wandered from one valley or woodland to another. When they came to a sheltered place, where there was pure running water, and where plenty of game and wood were to be found, they would build their lodges and light their council fires.

There they might camp for one moon, or for many moons. As long as their arrows brought game on the hunting trails near, they would not break camp. But if game grew scarce, or if for any reason they did not like the campground, they would move farther on.

Sometimes they would go several days' journey, before they found a camping place they liked.

The first thing that was done in making a camp was to secure fire and light the council fire. This fire was always kept burning. It never went out while they remained.

The Indians loved the fire. It was the gift of the Great Spirit. It kept them warm and cooked their food by day, and protected them by night.

A line of fires was kept burning around the camp. This protected the Indians from the wild animals. All animals fear and are yet charmed by fire. They might prowl and howl all night long outside the fire ring, but never would they attempt to come within that ring. There the Indians could sleep in peace, guarded by the spirits of the fire.

The Indian that could make fire first became a chief and leader. When it was decided to camp at a certain place, a signal would be given. At this the young braves would leap into the woods, to see which one first could bring back fire. Each had his own secret way of making it. Usually a bowstring was twisted about a fire stick, and the stick was turned rapidly in a groove. In a few seconds, smoke would rise from the sawdust that formed. After a little fanning, a flame would leap forth.

The Indian whose brain and hand worked swiftest and surest was the smartest and best man. He became a Firemaker, and was made a chief of the tribe. He could do something that the rest could not—at least he had proved himself to be more skillful. Such a man, it was thought, had a better understanding of all things, and therefore could tell the rest of the tribe what ought to be done.

He no longer was just a man who ate and slept, walked and ran. He was a man with a mind. He could think and could do things. So he became a Firemaker chief, and he helped the tribe to think and do.

The Iroquois believe that there are three kinds of men: those that use the body only; those that use body and mind; and those that use body, mind, and spirit.

Now it happened that somtimes an Indian grew to be so kind and so great, that he could not only strike the fire we see, but the fire we do not see—the fire of love that burns in the hearts of people.

Fire Stick

When an Indian could strike this kind of fire, and warm the hearts not only of his own tribe but of all tribes, so that they came to love one another, he was a great chief, a Peacemaker chief. Such a man would go from tribe to tribe, teaching the people how they should do, so that all might live in peace and plenty, like brothers.

To be a Peacemaker was the highest seat an Indian could take. Few Indians became Peacemaker chiefs, and they were the great men of the tribe.

Indian women might also become Peacemakers. At one time the Iroquois had a Peace Wigwam, where all disputes and quarrels were settled.

The most beautiful, just, and fair-minded woman of all the tribes was chosen to sit in this wigwam. It was her duty to tend the Peace fire, and to see that it never went out. She also kept a pot of hominy always steaming over the fire.

If two Indians had a dispute, it was the custom for them to run to the Peacemaker's wigwam. They entered from opposite sides. Inside the wigwam, a deerskin curtain separated them from each other.

The Peacemaker would listen to the grievance of the one and then to that of the other. Then she would draw aside the curtain, get the enemies together, and settle the dispute with justice.

The two would then eat of the hominy, and depart in peace—no longer enemies, but friends.

No nation could fight another nation without the consent of the Peacemaker. Because the peacewomen were wise, and just, and kind, and taught men to love, not fight each other, the Iroquois were for many years at peace.

But one day, it is said, a Peacewoman proved untrue to her trust. She thought more of her own happiness than that of the nation.

Peace Wigwam

This woman was very beautiful, and the people loved her. For some time she sat in the Peace Wigwam, and tended faithfully the Peace fire.

One day an Oneida and a Cayuga chief fell to quarreling. They sought the Peace Wigwam. As they entered and saw the young Peacewoman tending the fire, each thought he had never seen a woman so beautiful.

Into the heart of each there leaped the desire that she might tend his wigwam fire.

The Peacemaker listened to the quarrel of the young chiefs and settled it justly. Then each tried to persuade her to leave the Peace fire and return with him to his lodge. But the Peacemaker said, "No, I must tend the fire, it must be kept burning." The chiefs departed with heavy hearts.

But the Oneida chief could not forget the beautiful woman. When a moon had passed, he returned to the Peace Wigwam. This time he persuaded the Peacemaker to leave her fire and return with him to sit at his wigwam door.

The Peace fire flickered and went out. The Iroquois again went on the warpath, and for many, many moons, they fought and suffered and died.

Iroquois Wonder Stories

How the White Man Came

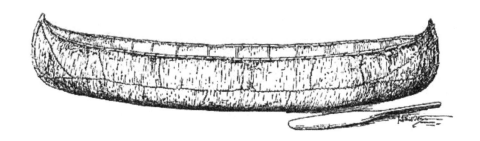

Long, long before Columbus came to America, the Indians were here. They were the first and only real Americans.

These Children of the Sun, as they called themselves, ranged from the Big Sea Water on the east to the Big Sea Water on the west.

Happy and free as the sunlight and air about them, they ran through wide forests all their own, or plied their bark canoes up and down the streams.

Then the Indian had a dream. This was long before Columbus dreamed his dream of the Western World.

In his dream the Indian saw a great White Bird coming out of the east. Its wings were stretched wide to the north and south. With great strength and speed, it swept toward the setting sun.

In fear and wonder the Indian watched this giant White Bird appear and disappear. He knew its meaning, and the Indian's heart was sad.

Then the White man came. From the Big Sea Water on the east he came, in his great white-winged canoe. With one hand pointing to the Great Spirit, and with the other extended to the Indian he came. He asked for a small seat. A seat the size of a buffalo skin would be quite large enough for him, he said.

In the name of the Great Spirit, the Indians greeted the White man, and called him "brother." They gave him the seat he asked. They gave him a large buffalo skin also, and showed him where he could spread it by their council fire.

The White man took the buffalo skin. He thanked his Indian brother in the name of the Great Spirit. Then he began to cut the skin into many, many small strips.

When the whole buffalo skin had been cut into narrow strips, he tied the strips together. They made a long cord that would reach over a long trail.

In amazement the Indians watched the White man while he measured off a seat as long and as broad as this cord would reach around. The "small seat," the size of a buffalo skin, became a tract of land.

Soon the White man asked for another seat—this time his seat took in the Indians' lodges and camp fire. He asked the Indians if they would move on a few arrow flights. This they did.

Then the White man wanted another seat. Each time it took a larger skin for him to sit upon. This time the skin stretched so far that it covered a part of the Indians' hunting and fishing grounds.

Again the Indians moved on. Again the White man followed. Each time his seat grew larger, until the Indian had a place but the size of a buffalo skin on which to sit.

Thus it was that the White man came. Like a great White Bird that swept from the Big Sea Water on the east to the Big Sea Water on the west, the White man came; and he drove the Indian from the rising to the setting sun.

Why the Eagle Defends Americans

Many, many moons before the White man came, a little Indian boy was left in the woods. It was in the days when animals and men understood each other better than they do now.

An old mother bear found the little Indian boy.

She felt very sorry for him. She told the little boy not to cry, for she would take him home with her. She had a nice wigwam in the hollow of a big tree.

Old Mother Bear had two cubs of her own, but she had a place between her great paws for a third. She took the little papoose, and she hugged him warm and close. She fed him as she did her own little cubs.

The boy grew strong. He was very happy with his adopted mother and brothers. They had a warm lodge in the hollow of the great tree. As they grew older, Mother Bear found for them all the honey and nuts that they could eat.

From sunrise to sunset, the little Indian boy played with his cub brothers. He did not know that he was different from them. He thought he was a little bear, too. All day long, the boy and the little bears played and had a good time. They rolled, and tumbled, and wrestled in the forest leaves. They chased one another up and down the bear tree.

Sometimes they had a matched game of hug, for every little bear must learn to hug. The one who could hug the longest and the tightest won the game.

Old Mother Bear watched her three dear children at their play. She would have been content and happy, but for one thing. She was afraid some harm would come to the boy. Never could she quite forget the bear hunters. Several times they had scented her tree, but the wind had thrown them off the trail.

Once, from her bear-tree window, she had thrown out rabbit hairs as she saw them coming. The wind had blown the rabbit hairs toward the hunters. As they fell near the hunters, they had suddenly changed into rabbits and the hunters had given chase.

At another time, Mother Bear tossed some partridge feathers to the wind as the hunters drew near her tree. A flock of partridges went whirring into the woods with a great noise, and the hunters ran after them.

But on this day, Mother Bear's heart was heavy. She knew that now the big bear hunters were coming. No rabbits or partridges could lead these hunters from the bear trail, for they had dogs with four eyes. (Foxhounds have a yellow spot over each eye which makes them seem double-eyed.) These dogs were never known to miss a bear tree. Sooner or later they would scent it.

Mother Bear thought she might be able to save herself and her cubs. But what would become of the boy? She loved him too much to let the bear hunters kill him.

Just then, the porcupine, the Chief of the animals, passed by the bear tree. Mother Bear saw him. She put her head out the bear-tree window and called to him. He came and sat under the bear-tree window, and listened to Mother Bear's story of her fears for the boy.

26

When she had finished, Chief Porcupine said he would call a council of the animals, and see if they could save the boy.

Now the Chief had a big voice. As soon as he raised his voice, even the animals away on the longest trails heard. They ran at once and gathered under the council tree. There was a loud roar, and a great flapping of wings, for the birds came too.

Chief Porcupine told them about the fears of Mother Bear, and of the danger to the boy.

"Now," said the Chief, "which one of you will take the boy, and save him from the bear hunters?"

It happened that some of the animals present were jealous of man. These animals had held more than one secret council, to plan how they could do away with the boy. They said he was becoming too powerful. He knew all they knew—and more.

The beaver did not like man, because men could build better houses than he.

The fox said that man had stolen his cunning, and could now outwit him.

The wolf and the panther objected to man, because he could conceal himself and spring with greater surety than they.

The raccoon said that man was more daring, and could climb higher than he.

The deer complained that man could outrun him.

So when Chief Porcupine asked who would take the boy and care for him, each of these animals in turn said that he would gladly do so.

Mother Bear sat by and listened as each offered to care for the boy. She did not say anything, but she was thinking hard—for a bear. At last she spoke.

To the beaver she said, "You cannot take the boy; you will drown him on the way to your lodge." To the fox she said, "You cannot take him; you would teach him to cheat and steal, while pretending to be a friend; neither can the wolf or the panther have him, for they are counting on having something good to eat. You, deer, you have no home, you are a tramp. And you, raccoon, I cannot trust, for you would coax him to climb so high that he would fall and die. No, none of you can have the boy."

Now a great bird that lives in the sky had flown into the council tree while the animals were speaking. But they had not seen him.

When Mother Bear had spoken, this wise old eagle flew down, and said, "Give the boy to me, Mother Bear. No bird is as swift and strong as the eagle. I will protect him. On my great wings I will bring him far away from the bear hunters to the wigwam of an Indian friend, where a little Indian boy is wanted."

Mother Bear looked into the eagle's keen eyes. She saw that he could see far.

Then she said, "Take him, eagle. I trust him to you. I know you will protect the boy."

The eagle spread wide his great wings. Mother Bear placed the boy on his back, and away they soared, far from the council woods.

As he promised, the eagle left the boy at the door of a wigwam where a little Indian boy was wanted.

This was the first young American to be saved by an American eagle.

The boy grew to be a noble chief and a great hunter. No hunter could hit a bear trail so soon as he, for he knew just where and how to find the bear trees. But never was he known to cut down a bear tree, or to kill a bear.

However, there were many wolf, panther, and deerskins that hung in his lodge. The hunter's wife sat and made warm coats from the fox and beaver skins which the hunter father brought in from the chase. But never was the hunter, his wife, or his children seen to wear a bear-skin coat.

How the Turkey Buzzard Got His Suit

It was a long, long time ago, when the earth was very young. Trees and flowers were growing everywhere, but there were no birds. One morning the Great Spirit drew back the blanket from the door of his wigwam in the sky.

He looked upon the earth and smiled, for he saw that his work was good.

"Today," he thought, "I will make big birds to fly in and out among the beautiful trees and flowers of the earth. They shall sing as they fly."

Then the Great Spirit spoke, and the tree tops were full of birds—but they had no feathers.

All day he watched them fly and listened to their songs. But their naked bodies and long legs did not please him. Before the sun had set, he had made feathered suits of every size and color to cover them.

That night, as the birds hid their heads under their wings, the Great Spirit spoke to them. He told about the feathered suits he had made for them, and where these suits could be found.

A council was called the next day by the birds. They chose **Gah gah go wah**, the Turkey Buzzard, to get the suits. He could fly over a long trail and not be tired.

The birds told him that if he would go, he could have the first choice of the suits of feathers, but he must try on no suit more than once.

Turkey Buzzard promised and set out toward the setting sun. Twice the sun set, and three times it rose, before he found the feathered suits. There were many of them, and they were very beautiful. He could not make up his mind which one he would like best to wear.

Then he remembered that he could try on each suit of feathers once. So he began to put them on.

The feathers of the first suit were too long. They trailed on the ground as he walked. Neither could he fly well in them. Turkey Buzzard laid that suit aside.

The next suit shone like gold. The feathers were a beautiful yellow. Turkey Buzzard put it on and strutted up and down the forest.

"Oh, how handsome I am!" he said. "But I must not keep this, for if I did, I should shine like the face of the Great Spirit, and all the other birds would see me."

He slipped off the suit of yellow feathers as quickly as possible.

A third suit was of pure white feathers. Turkey Buzzard thought it looked very beautiful and it was a perfect fit.

"But it will get dirty too soon," he said. "I will not choose this."

And this, too, was laid aside.

There were not enough feathers in the fourth suit. Turkey Buzzard shivered with cold. It was not warm enough. He would not have it.

There were too many feathers, and too many pieces, in the fifth suit. It took too much time to put it on. Turkey Buzzard did not want that.

So he went from one suit to another, trying on and taking off. Always he had some new fault to find. Something was wrong with each one. Nothing quite pleased him. No suit was just right.

At last there was but one suit left. It was not pretty. It was a plain, dull color—and very short of feathers at the neck and head. Turkey Buzzard put it on. He did not like it. It did not fit him well. It was cut too low in the neck. Turkey Buzzard thought it was the homeliest suit of all. But it was the last suit, so he kept it on.

Then **Gah gah go wah**, the Turkey Buzzard, gathered up the suits and flew back to the bird lodge. He still wore the plain, dull-colored suit.

The birds again called a council. Each was told to select a suit from those that **Gah gah go wah** had brought, and put it on. This they did.

Then the birds in their beautiful feathered suits began to walk and fly about the Turkey Buzzard, and to make fun of his plain, dull dress.

But **Gah gah go wah** held his head high. He walked proudly about among the birds. He looked with scorn on their beautiful suits. After a time he spoke.

He said, "**Gah gah go wah**, the Turkey Buzzard, does not want your suits. He had the pick of them all. He likes his own suit best."

Why the Partridge Drums

It was after the Great Spirit had made all the beautiful birds that the Evil Spirit came along. He saw the beautiful birds and heard their beautiful songs. He saw that the earth people liked the birds and liked to hear them sing.

Now the Evil Spirit did not wish people to be happy, so he said, "I will make a bird that will make people afraid. I will make a big bird that will not sing, but will make a great noise."

So the Evil Spirit went to work. In a short time he had made a big bird that could not sing, but could drum.

The big bird flew away into the wood. That night a drumming noise was heard in the wood. The people were afraid. They could not sleep, because of the noise.

In the morning, they went into the woods to search for the noise. Deep in the forest could still be heard that strange drumming. They followed it, until they came to a deep, dark place in the woods. There was a loud fluttering and whirring of wings and a great bird flew out from among them, along the ground and over the trees.

The people were afraid. They called to the Great Spirit to help them.

The Great Spirit was near. He heard their cry, and went after the bird, for he was very angry.

The Great Spirit said, "I will not have my people frightened by this great bird. It shall die."

The big bird gave the Great Spirit a long chase. At last the Great Spirit came upon it. He seized it, and threw it against a large tree.

As the big bird struck the tree, drops of blood flew in all directions. They changed into smaller birds that went whirring into the woods, just as the big bird had done. There they began to drum.

Like the big bird, these smaller birds like to startle people. They flutter out from under the leaves, and with a whirring noise they fly far into the wood. There they perch on an old log, or a rock, and drum with their wings.

Some of the earth people say they are drumming for their mates. But others still think that the birds drum to make people afraid.

So this is how the Indians say the partridges came to be. This is why they drum, and why some of the earth children still love to hunt partridges.

How the Indians Learned to Heal

A long, long time ago, some Indians were running along a trail that led to an Indian settlement. As they ran, a rabbit jumped from the bushes and sat before them.

The Indians stopped, for the rabbit still sat up before them and did not move from the trail. They shot their arrows at him, but the arrows came back unstained with blood.

A second time they drew their arrows. Now no rabbit was to be seen. Instead, an old man stood on the trail. He seemed to be weak and sick.

The old man asked them for food and a place to rest. They would not listen but went on to the settlement.

Slowly the old man followed them down the trail to the wigwam village. In front of each wigwam, he saw a skin placed on a pole. This he knew was the sign of the clan to which the dwellers in that wigwam belonged.

First he stopped at a wigwam where a wolf skin hung. He asked to enter, but they would not let him. They said, "We want no sick men here."

On he went toward another wigwam. Here a turtle's shell was hanging. But this family would not let him in.

He tried a wigwam where he saw a beaver skin. He was told to move on. The Indians who lived in a wigwam where a deer skin was seen, were just as unkind. Nor was he permitted to enter wigwams where hung hawk, snipe, and heron skins.

At last he came to a wigwam where a bear skin hung.

"I will ask once more for a place to rest," he thought.

And here a kind old woman lived. She brought food for him to eat, and spread soft skins for him to lie upon.

The old man thanked her. He said that he was very sick. He told the woman what plants to gather in the wood to make him well again.

This she did, and soon he was healed. A few days later the old man was again taken sick. Again he told the woman what roots and leaves to gather. She did as she was told, and soon he was well.

Many times the old man fell sick. Each time he had a different sickness. Each time he told the woman what plants and herbs to find to cure him. Each time she remembered what she had been told.

Soon this woman of the Bear clan knew more about healing than all the other people.

One day, the old man told her that the Great Spirit had sent him to earth, to teach the Indian people the secrets of healing.

"I came, sick and hungry, to many a wigwam door. No blanket was drawn aside for me to pass in. You alone lifted the blanket from your wigwam door and asked me to enter. You are of the Bear clan, therefore all other clans shall come to the Bear clan for help in sickness. You shall teach all the clans what plants, and roots, and leaves to gather, so the sick may be healed. The Bear shall be the greatest and strongest of the clans."

The Indian woman lifted her face to the Great Spirit to thank him for this great gift and knowledge of healing. When she turned again to the man, he had disappeared.

No one was there, but a rabbit was running swiftly down the trail.

Why Dogs Chase Foxes

A fox was running through the wood near a river. He had a fish in his mouth.

The fish had been stolen from an Indian who lived down the stream. The fox had been passing near the Indian's wigwam. He saw the fish hanging by the fire. It was cleaned and ready to cook.

"What a tasty breakfast!" thought the fox. "I think I will watch the man eat."

Soon the Indian went into the wigwam. The fox slipped up to the fire. He seized the fish, and ran away with it.

When the Indian came back, he had no breakfast. The fish was gone. No fox was to be seen.

The fox ran along, feeling very pleased with himself.

"What a cunning fox I am," he chuckled. "I will play another foxy trick. This time it shall be on the bear I see coming."

He ran up a tree that had been bent half way to earth by the West Wind. There he began to eat his fish. He smacked his lips so loudly that the bear heard him.

The bear stopped under the tree, and asked, "What are you eating that tastes so good?"

For answer the fox threw down a bit of the fish. The bear smacked his lips and cried, "More! More!"

"Go to the river, swim out to the big log, and catch your own fish," called the fox. "It's very easy! Just drop your tail into the water. Hold it there till a fish comes along and bites, then pull it up. That is the way I catch my fish. You can catch all the fish you want with your own tail."

The bear hurried on to the river. He swam to the log and dropped his tail into the water, as the fox had advised.

All day he sat and fished with his tail—for bears then had very long tails.

The sun set, but no fish had pulled his tail. All night the bear sat on the log and fished. Cold North Wind blew his breath over the water. The river grew still and white.

Toward morning, the bear felt that his tail was getting very heavy. Now at last he was sure he had a fish. He tried to pull it up. But alas! His tail was frozen fast in the ice.

Then the fox came along. He laughed long and loudly at the bear, and asked if the fishing was good.

Some dogs heard the fox, and came running through the thick underbrush. They saw the fox and started after him.

The fox slyly led them on to the frozen river toward the bear. The bear saw them coming, and called to the fox to go around some other way. The fox made believe he did not hear, and came straight on to the bear to ask him what he had said.

The dogs leaped upon the bear. The bear struggled. He gave one great pull, and freed himself from the ice. He struck at the dogs so fiercely with his great paws, that they soon left him, and went on after the fox. Dogs have been running after foxes ever since.

When the bear got his breath, he stood up and looked around at his tail. He found he had only a small piece left. Most of his tail had been left in the ice.

This is why bears have short tails, and why dogs still love to chase the fox.

Why Hermit Thrush is so Shy

Some moons after the council when the birds chose their feathered suits, a second council was called. The purpose of this council was to see which bird could fly to heaven and bring a song to earth.

When all the birds had arrived and were perched upon the council tree, the wise old owl spoke.

"Listen friends and brothers," said the owl. "Many of you have strong wings, but your voices are not beautiful. High, high up in the sky, a long trail beyond the clouds, is the Happy Hunting Ground.

"There live all our brothers of the wood, whom the Great Spirit has called. They sing songs more beautiful than any heard on earth.

"The bird that can fly beyond the clouds will hear that singing. He shall bring a song to earth. Who will fly the Great Sky Trail, and bring a song to earth? Who-whoo! Who-whoo! Who-whoo!"

At this, all the birds that were swift of wing flew high in the air. They circled round and round to show their skill. Then they disappeared in the clouds.

But one by one they dropped to earth; for when they had reached the Great Sky Trail beyond the clouds, they were too tired to take it.

At last the eagle arose and stretched his great wings.

"Listen," he said, "for the Chief of Birds speaks. No other bird is so swift and so strong as the eagle. He has circled the earth. He has flown to the rim of the world. The eagle will fly the Great Sky Trail and bring the song to earth."

A little brown thrush sat near the eagle.

"Oh," he thought, "how I would like to bring that song to earth!"

But he was so small, and his wings were so tired!

Then an idea popped into the little brown head of the thrush. He hopped softly to the back of the eagle, and hid in the thick feathers near the neck. So small and light was the thrush, that the eagle did not feel his weight. He did not know that the little brown thrush was on his back—and the other birds did not tell him.

The eagle spread his great wings. Up, and up, and up, they soared. The council wood became a little speck and then was seen no more. Over, and under, and through the clouds, on and on and on they sailed, along the Great Sky Trail.

At last the eagle's strength began to fail. He could go no further. The great wings of the chief of birds could beat the air no longer. They fell at his side.

The little brown thrush felt the eagle quiver and begin to drop toward the earth.

Then away flew the little brown thrush. The air was so light it seemed easy to fly. On and on he went, for he was not tired. He had had a ride almost to heaven.

"Now," he thought, "I will go on and get the song."

For some time, the little brown thrush flew along the Great Sky Trail. All at once the air seemed full of song. He knew he was nearing the Happy Hunting Ground.

He listened. One song seemed more beautiful to him than the rest. Again and again he listened. He caught the notes. He sang them many times, until he was sure that he could carry the song to earth.

Then down, and down, and down, he floated, through clouds and storms and sunshine, back to Mother Earth.

Very happy, he flew toward the council wood. He was so full of his beautiful song and the wonderful Sky Trail, he thought he must pour out his song at once.

But when he reached the council wood, he dared not open his mouth! He remembered that he had stolen his ride part way to heaven—and he knew the other birds knew it.

But that song! He must sing it! He thought his throat would burst, if he did not sing!

So the little brown thrush flew off by himself, into a deep, dark part of the wood. There, hidden by the brush and the bushes, he poured forth the song he had heard on the Great Sky Trail.

Men hearing it today say, "Listen, a hermit thrush! What a beautiful song! But he is such a shy bird, one seldom can catch a glimpse of him."

They do not know why he keeps so close under cover.

How Good and Evil Came to Be

Every boy has wondered how there came to be two of him. Every girl has puzzled over how she happened to be twins. Sometimes she is a good girl—sometimes a naughty one. The Indians say this is how it happened.

The world was very young. There was no earth, only a cloud-like sea. The sea was filled with water animals, and water birds flew over it. All was dark. Light had not yet come. Then the cloud-sea began to call for light.

The Great Spirit heard, and said, "It shall be so. I will make a new place for man to live in." The Great Spirit called the beautiful Sky Mother to Him. Her face was like the sun, she was so light of heart.

The Great Spirit told the Sky Mother to look down. She, too, heard the cloud-sea calling, and she said, "I will go."

As she began to descend, the animals saw her coming. "See the light," they cried. "Where will it rest?"

One of the water animals said, "I will go to the bottom of the sea and get something for it to rest on." He went down, but he never came back. Other animals followed him. But they, too, did not come back.

Then the muskrat said, "I will go. I will be the earth bringer." He returned, with some mud in his mouth and claws. "It will grow fast," he cried, in a weak voice. "Who will carry it?"

The turtle offered his back. As the muskrat placed the mud on the turtle's shell he died. But the beaver came and slapped the mud down with his tail.

The mud on the turtle's back grew very fast. Soon it was a small island. The turtle became the earth bearer. He has continued to hold up the earth ever since.

Now, when the sea rises in great waves, or the earth shakes, the Indians say, "The turtle is stretching. He is wiggling his back!"

41

Now, since there was a place for the light to rest on, the birds flew up to meet it. They found that the light was the beautiful Sky Mother.

Then the birds spread wide their great wings, and bore the Sky Mother through the air to the cloud-sea. They placed her on the island on the turtle's back. There the Sky Mother had rested some time, when she felt something stirring beneath her heart. She heard voices. One was soft and kind and full of love, the other was harsh and quarrelsome.

Soon the Sky Mother looked into the faces of the first-born of earth, for she had borne the twin brothers, the spirits of Good and Evil. As she looked into the face of the Good Mind, she said, "You shall be called the Light One."

Then she looked into the face of his brother, and said, "You shall be named the Dark One."

The island became a beautiful land.

The twin brother Light One grew up happy, loving, peaceful, and kind. He wanted to make the new land the most beautiful place in which to live. The twin brother Dark One grew up sullen, quarrelsome, hateful, and unkind. He tried to make the land the worst place in which to live.

From his mother's beautiful face the Light One made the sun. He set it in the eastern sky that it might shine forever. Then the Dark One put darkness in the west to drive the sun from the sky.

The Light One gave his mother's body to the earth, the Great Mother from which springs all life. He made great mountains, and covered them with forests from which beautiful rivers ran. The Dark One threw down the mountains, gnarled the forests, and bent the rivers which his brother had made.

Every beautiful thing which the good brother Light One made, the bad brother Dark One tried to destroy and ruin.

And because the first-born of earth were the twin spirits, the Good Mind and the Evil Mind, there has been a good and bad spirit born into every boy and girl who has come into the world since...so the Indians say.

How a Boy was Cured of Boasting

There was once an Indian boy, who thought he knew more and could do more than anyone else. He was so proud of himself that he walked around like a great chief, who wears a war shirt with many scalp locks on it.

The other Indian boys and girls called him Spread Feather, because he strutted about like a big turkey or a peacock.

One day, Spread Feather was playing ball with the other boys. Not once had he failed to drive or catch the ball with his crosse stick. Twice he had thrown the ball with such force that someone had been hurt.

Spread Feather grew more and more pleased with himself, as he played. He began to use tricks and to talk very large.

"No one can play ball as I," he said. "I can catch the swiftest ball that can be thrown. I can throw the ball to the sky. I can run faster than the deer."

Spread Feather boasted so loudly that a rabbit heard him. The rabbit came out of the bushes and sat up on his hind legs. He watched Spread Feather play, and listened to his boasting.

Soon a strange boy was standing where the rabbit had been. The stranger said to Spread Feather, "I would like to play ball with you."

"Come on, then!" taunted the boastful boy. "Spread Feather will show the strange ball player how to catch a ball."

They began to play.

The stranger could run like a deer. The balls he threw were so swift and so curved that Spread Feather could not see them. He could not catch one. They seemed to come from the sky.

At last one ball hit Spread Feather on the mouth and he fell to the ground. His face was red with anger, and his lips were red with blood.

He sprang to his feet and shouted to the stranger, "Though I do not like the taste of your ball, I can still throw you."

"Very well, then," said the stranger. "We will have a game of 'Catch as catch can.'" This is the Indian name for a game of wrestling.

Spread Feather set his feet very hard on the ground.

"My legs are as strong as the legs of a bear," he boasted.

They began to wrestle. Soon Spread Feather's arms fell at his sides. He panted for air. He had no breath and no strength.

The stranger picked Spread Feather up and tossed him over his head like a ball. The boy fell without a word.

When Spread Feather opened his eyes, a rabbit sprang into the bushes.

All night, Spread Feather lay and thought, and thought. He was too weak and too sore to go back to his wigwam. Nor was he eager to meet the other boys.

At sunrise a rabbit hopped near. The rabbit slyly suggested that he might like to play another game of ball.

The boy sat up and said to the rabbit, "Spread Feather is no more. He no longer struts like a turkey. He has nothing to say. He will win a new name. It will not be Spread Feather."

Why the Cuckoo is so Lazy

The land was lean and hungry. The Old Man of the North Lodge had breathed upon the valley. His breath had frozen the corn, and there was no bread for the people.

The Indian hunters took to the chase. They followed every track of deer or rabbit. If their arrows brought them meat, they threw it over their shoulders and ran to the village, so the hungry women and children might eat.

But one Indian remained in his wigwam. He sat by the fire with his wife and child, and waited for the hunters to bring game.

This man refused to go on the hunt. He was lazy. All day he sat by the fire and smoked his pipe. Once in a while, he would stir the water in the kettle which he kept boiling for the meat that he hoped the hunters might bring. Whenever the child, his little son, begged him for food, he would say, "It isn't done yet."

At last the little Indian boy grew so sick and faint for want of food that he cried aloud.

The lazy Indian father was angry. He seized the pudding stick, and struck the child to the ground. Instantly a bird flew up and perched on the pole over the fire, from which the kettle hung.

"Now it's done!" said the bird solemnly, for it did not seem to have a light heart like other birds.

Now, strange as it may seem, this father was no longer cruel and lazy. His lazy spirit seemed to have gone. He wanted to go at once on the chase, and hunt food for his wife and little boy.

"Tonight you shall have deer meat to eat," he said, as he spread a soft skin by the fire, for the boy to lie on. Then he turned to place the child on the skin—but no boy was there. He had no son. Only that strange bird perched, joyless and alone, over the fire, on the pole from which the kettle hung.

"Now it's done!" the bird cried again, and with that it flew out of the wigwam.

That spring the Indians discovered a new bird in the woods. The bird was too lazy to build a real nest.

This bird did not weave together twigs and moss, leaves and ferns, bits of hair and thistledown, to make a cozy, warm, safe nest for its eggs and young, as did the other birds. This bird would lay its eggs anywhere. Wherever a few sticks lay crosswise in a track, or in a little hollow of the ground, or where some twigs or dried ferns were caught loosely in a bush, there this lazy bird would lay its eggs and rear its young.

It was too lazy to build a real nest that was safe and warm for its little ones.

The Indians called the bird "the cuckoo." But only one Indian knew how the cuckoo came to be, and why it is too lazy to build a real nest.

How the Raccoon Outwitted the Fox

A wise old raccoon sat up in a tree near the river where the bear lost his tail. The raccoon saw the fox play his foxy trick on the bear, and he did not like it.

"The fox is getting a big head," said the raccoon. "This must not be. His head must be made smaller. Some of the foxiness must be taken out of it. He is getting too foxy. He thinks he has the cunning of all the animals, and that no one can outwit him. Someone must play a 'fox' trick on him."

Not many days later, the raccoon saw the fox coming down the trail. The raccoon was eating some juicy yellow apples that he had found on a tree not far away. As soon as he saw the fox, he ran up a tree, and began to smack his lips as the fox had done to tempt the bear.

The fox stopped under the tree, just as the bear had stopped.

"What tastes so good?" he asked.

For answer the raccoon threw down an apple to the fox, just as the fox had thrown the piece of fish down to the bear.

The fox took the apple and ate it.

"Fine! Fine!" said the fox, when he had finished the last mouthful. "Where did you get it?"

The raccoon then told the fox how to find the apple tree. He must follow the trail along the river, down to the pine bluff. Then he must climb the bluff and run toward the setting sun, until he came to an open field. In the center of the field a great apple tree stood filled with juicy yellow apples.

"But you can climb the tree and pick your own apples. How can I get them off the tree?" whined the fox.

"Oh, that's easy," said the raccoon. "Just back off two bow shots from the tree and lower your head. Run hard and butt the tree with your head. You have such a big head, it will shake the tree so hard that all the apples will fall at once. Do as I tell you, and you will have all the apples you want for a long time."

The fox thanked the raccoon and started at once.

He found the apple tree, just as the raccoon had said.

"What a fine open place to run in," thought the fox. "I will get such a fine start that when I hit the tree it will shake the world."

In his mind, he already began to see the apples falling, like pine needles, and to feel the earth shake under his feet.

The fox did as the raccoon had told him. One arrow flight he backed off, then another. Then he closed his eyes, lowered his head, and ran swiftly over the thick grass. He struck the tree as hard as he could, with his big head.

Not an apple fell, but a dazed, foolish-looking fox fell to the ground.

Next morning as the sun rose, a shame-faced fox was seen running toward the woods beyond the pine bluff. He carried his head low, and he seemed to be playing no foxy tricks.

Why the Goldfinches Look Like the Sun

It was some moons after the raccoon outwitted the fox, before they again met. The raccoon was hurrying by, when the fox saw him.

Now the fox had not forgotten the trick the raccoon had played on him. His head was still sore from that great thump against the apple tree. So the fox started running after the raccoon. He was gaining, and would have caught him, if they had not come to a tall pine tree.

The raccoon ran to the very tiptop of the pine tree. There he was safe, because the fox could not climb.

The fox lay down on the soft pine needles and waited for the raccoon to come down. The raccoon stayed up in the pine tree so long that the fox grew tired and sleepy. He closed his eyes and thought he would take a short nap.

The raccoon watched, until he saw that the fox was sound asleep. Then he took some of the pitch from the pine tree in his mouth. He ran down the tree and rubbed the pitch over the eyes of the sleeping fox.

The fox awoke. He sprang up and tried to seize the raccoon, but he could not see what he was doing. The lids of his eyes were held fast with the pine gum and he could not open them.

The raccoon laughed at the fox's plight, then ran and left him.

The fox lay for some time under the tree. The pine gum, as it dried, held the lids of his eyes closer and closer shut. He thought he should never again see the sun.

Some birds were singing nearby. He called them, and told them of his plight. He asked if they would be so kind as to pick open his eyes.

The birds flew off and told the other birds. Soon many of the little dark songsters flew back to where the fox lay. Then peck, peck, peck, went the little bills on the eyelids of the fox. Bit by bit they carefully pecked away the pine gum. If one grew tired, another bird would take its place.

At last the fox saw a streak of light. Soon the lid of one eye flew open, then the other. The sun was shining, and the world looked very beautiful to the fox, as he opened his eyes.

He was very grateful to the little birds for bringing him light. He told them to ask what they would, and he would give it to them.

The little birds said, "We do not like the plain, dark suits which the Turkey Buzzard brought us. Make us look like the sun we have brought to you."

The fox looked about him. Beautiful yellow flowers were growing near. He pressed some of the sun color from them, and with the tip of his tail as a brush, he began to paint the dark little birds like the sun.

The birds fluttered so with joy, he thought he would paint the bodies first. Before he could brush the wings and tails with the sun paint, each little bird had darted away, like a streak of sunshine. So happy and light of heart were the birds, that they could not wait for the fox to finish the painting.

This is why goldfinches are yellow like the sun. It is why they have black wings and tails, why they flutter so with joy, and why they never finish their song.

What the Ash and the Maple Learned

Long ago, birds, trees, animals, and men knew the language of the other, and all could talk together.

In those days, the trees of the forest grew very large and strong. At last they came to know their strength too well. They became selfish, and proud, and quarrelsome. Each tree boasted that he was the greatest and strongest. Each one struggled to gain for himself the most earth, the best air, the brightest sun. No tree had a thought for the other.

One day the trunk of a great Maple tried to crowd out an Ash. The Ash, of course, thought he had as much right to stand there as the Maple, and he said he would not move a limb.

"Get out of my way," cried the Maple. "I am greater than you, and of more use to man; for I furnish the sweet water for him to drink."

"Indeed, I will not!" said the Ash. "I am greater than you, and of more use to man than you; for I furnish the tough wood from which he makes his bow."

At this the trees fell to wrestling. Back and forth, in and out they swayed, each trying to throw the other. They forgot that they were brothers in the wood.

Then the South Wind came along. He heard the loud voices and stopped to find out what the quarrel was about.

"I am greater than you, for I furnish the sweet water for man to drink," cried the angry voice of the Maple, as he threw his huge trunk against the Ash.

"No, you are not," retorted the Ash, and he sent the Maple back with a great push of his strong elbow. "I am greater than you, for I furnish the tough wood from which he makes his bow."

For a time, the South Wind watched them writhe and twist and try to throw each other to the ground. Then he said, softly, "You, O Maple, do not cause the sweet water to flow for man; nor do you, O Ash, make your wood to grow pliant and tough for his bow."

"Who does, then?" they asked defiantly.

"Listen," said the South Wind, "and you shall hear."

Then the Maple and Ash forgot their quarrel. They bent their heads so low and close to listen that an arm of the Maple slipped through an arm of the Ash.

And as they stood thus listening, each with an arm locked in an arm of the other, the South Wind gently swayed them to and fro. Then a voice was heard, singing, "*San noh-eh! San noh-eh! San noh-eh!*" which means, "The Mother of all things."

Thus it was that the Ash and the Maple learned that it was Mother Earth who gave them their life, and power, and strength, and that they were brothers, because they had one Mother.

The Ash and the Maple whispered the secret to the birds. The birds came and listened to the voice, and went and told the animals. The animals came and listened, and went and told men. And thus all the earth children learned that there is one Great Mother of every living thing, and that all are brothers.

And now, whenever two trees lock arms lovingly, and the South Wind sways them gently to and fro, that same voice may be heard, singing, "*San noh-eh! San noh-eh! San noh-eh!*

How the Woman Overcame the Bear

An Indian woman built a wigwam in the deep wood. She was a brave woman. She had no fear.

One night, she heard something coming along the trail. Thump, thump, thump, it came, to the very door of her wigwam.

There was a knock.

"Come in," said the woman, but no one entered.

Again there came a knock.

Again the woman called, "Come in." Again the latch was not lifted.

A third time the knock came. A third time the woman called, "Come in," but no one entered.

Then the strange thump, thump, thump, was heard going down the trail.

The next night, the same thing happened. Soon after dark, the woman heard the thump, thump, thump, coming along the trail. Up to the very door of the wigwam it came.

Three times, a knock, knock, knock, was heard as before. Three times the woman answered, "Come in," but no one entered.

Then the same strange thump, thump, thump, was heard going down the trail again.

The third night, the woman thought she would find out who was calling. She stood for a long time, with her hand on the latch.

At last she heard the visitor coming. Thump, thump, thump, it came along the trail. There were three knocks.

"Come in," called the woman, but the latch did not move in her hand. She waited. Again came the knocks.

This time she threw the door open wide, and there stood a great black bear. He showed his sharp teeth and growled, "Are you at home?"

The woman looked him straight in the eye and replied, "I am at home."

At once the bear turned on his heel and went down the trail, as fast as he could go.

Never again did the woman hear that strange thump, thump, thump. And never again did the bear knock to see if she was at home.

Why the Woodpecker Bores for its Food

Once upon a time, the Great Spirit left the Happy Hunting Ground and came to earth. He took the form of a poor, hungry man. He went from wigwam to wigwam, asking for food.

Sometimes he found the Indians sitting around the fire, telling stories and talking of the Great Spirit. Then the man would pass by unseen.

One day, he came to a wigwam in which a woman was baking cakes.

"I am very hungry," the man said. "Will you please give me a cake?"

The woman looked at the man, and then at the cake. She saw that it was too large to give away.

She said, "I will not give you this cake, but I will bake you one, if you will wait."

The hungry man said, "I will wait."

Then the woman took a small piece of dough and made it into a cake and baked it. But when she took this cake from the coals, it was larger than the first.

Again the woman looked at her cake. Again she saw it was too large to give away. Again she said, "I will not give you this one, but I will bake you one, if you will wait."

Again the man said, "I will wait."

This time the woman took a very, very, tiny bit of dough, and made it into a cake.

"Surely, this will be small enough to give away," she thought, yet when baked it was larger than both the others.

The woman stood and looked at the three cakes. Each was too large to give away.

"I will not give you any of the cakes," she said to the man. "Go to the woods, and find your food in the bark of trees."

Then the man stood up and threw off his ragged blanket and worn moccasins. His face shone like the sun, and he was very beautiful. The woman shrank into the shadow of the wigwam. She could not look upon his face, for the light.

"I am the Great Spirit," said he, "and you are a selfish woman. Women should be kind, and generous, and unselfish. You shall no longer be a woman and live in a warm wigwam, with plenty of cakes to bake. *You* shall go to the forest and hunt *your* food in the bark of trees. Summer and winter, you shall eat worms of the same size as the cake you would have made for me."

The woman began to grow smaller and smaller. Feathers grew upon her body, and wings sprang from it. The Great Spirit touched her head, and it became red.

"Always shall you wear this red hood," he said, "as a mark of your shame. Always shall you hide from man. Always shall you hunt for little worms, the size of the cake you made for me."

At this a sharp cry was heard, and a bird flew into the fireplace of the wigwam, and up the chimney. As it passed out of the chimney, the soot left those long streaks of black which we see now on the woodpecker's back.

Ever since then, this woodpecker has had a red head, and has been hiding from man on the farther side of the tree trunk, and boring in the bark for little worms.

Why the Ice Roof Fell

A great many winters ago, there lived at the foot of a certain lake a tribe of wicked Indians. These Indians were so fierce, and warlike, and wasteful, they went about destroying everything.

They cut a tract of beautiful forest trees, for no good purpose. They tore up shrubs and plants that gave them food and medicine. They shot their arrows into every bird or animal they saw, just for sport.

The great trees—their silent brothers of the wood—trembled and sighed when they heard these Indians coming. The squirrels darted into hollow trees, and birds flew in alarm at their footsteps. The deer and rabbit ran from the trail.

At last the Great Spirit became very angry with this tribe. Always he had taught the Indians never to kill an animal, unless for food and protection; never to fell a tree, unless for fuel or shelter; never to dig up shrubs or plants, unless for some good use.

"All life," the Great Spirit had said, "is sacred and beautiful. It must not be wasted."

And never before had he known the Indians to waste the beautiful living things about them. The Great Spirit was very sad.

The ice formed very thick on the lake that winter.

One night, there came a great storm of wind and rain. The ice broke loose from the shores, and the wind blew it down the lake. At the foot of the lake, a mass of ice was piled high over the shore, where these wasteful Indians lived.

Like a giant roof, the ice spread over the little Indian village lying there asleep, but the Indians did not know. They slept on, unaware of their danger, for a deep, heavy sleep had come upon them.

Just as the sun rose, the ice roof gave way and fell upon the sleeping Indians, crushing them in their wigwams.

The waste they had brought upon their brothers of the wood had brought punishment upon them. The Great Spirit had destroyed these wicked Indians, that the good Indians might keep his world beautiful.

Ever after, as long as the Indians occupied the country, before the White man came, no trees were felled, and no animals or birds were killed, unless for some wise and useful purpose.

Why the Chipmunk has Black Stripes

At one time, the animals had tribes and chiefs, like men. It was when the porcupine was chief, that a council was called.

A great fire was lighted, for it was night. When all the animals were seated around the fire, the porcupine spoke.

"Friends," he said, "we have met here to settle a great question: 'Shall we have night all the time, or day?'" At this, all the animals began to talk at once. There was great confusion. The night animals kept shouting, "Night, night! Always night!" Other animals cried, "Day, day! Always day!" Still others called for "Day and night!"

There was so much noise that it could not be decided what was best.

At last the animals grew tired of calling. One by one the voices grew fainter, and the shouting ceased. Of the night animals, the voice of the bear alone was heard. He had a big voice and still kept calling, "Night, night! Always night!"

The animals who wanted day all the time, and those who wanted day and night, also became quiet—all except the chipmunk.

He chattered on, "We will have light—and then night. We will have light—and then night. Chee, chee, chee!"

Then the bear, too, became tired. He was fat and lazy, and so sleepy! He thought he would take a short nap.

But all night long the wide-awake little chipmunk kept up his song. Not for a moment did he stop to rest. Out of the dark came his voice, sure and cheery, "We will have light—and then night. We will have light—and then night! Chee, chee, chee!"

And before the animals knew it, the sun began to rise.

At the first rays of light, the bear sat up, blinked, and rubbed his eyes. He saw that while he had slept, light had indeed come. He knew that he and the night animals had been beaten in the council, and that the chipmunk and the animals who wanted day and night had won.

The bear was very angry. He struck at the chipmunk with his paw. But he was clumsy, and the chipmunk was spry!

The chipmunk laughed and sprang into a hole of a hollow tree nearby. But those black stripes on the chipmunk's back show where the paw of the black bear touched him as he slipped into the tree.

Ever since this council, and the little chipmunk called so long and loud for "light and night," we have had day and night.

How Two Indian Boys Settled a Quarrel

Flying Squirrel and Lightning Bow were two little Indian boys. They lived by Singing River, and they played from sunrise to sunset. They were as happy as the day was long.

In the summer, they fished and swam in Singing River, and they shot their arrows into chipmunk and woodpecker holes. Sometimes they played "Dodging Arrows," a game their mother had taught them when they were very young.

In the winter, they jumped into fleecy snowdrifts and rolled until their little bronze bodies took on a red-raspberry tint. Then they would send their snow-snakes skimming over the hard crust of snow.

Snow-snakes were small rods of wood, polished smooth with resin, oil, or wax. They could be thrown long distances. Long Moose—Lightning Bow and Flying Squirrel's father—could throw a snow-snake a mile and a half, over the crust of the snow. But the snow-snakes he used were eight feet long and tipped with lead.

It was the Moon of Berries. Six times Flying Squirrel and Lightning Bow had seen the Berry Moon hang her horn in the night sky. And not once in all their lives had they quarreled.

One morning, Flying Squirrel and Lightning Bow planned a foot race. Seven times they were to run. Three times, Flying Squirrel had made the goal first. Three times, Lightning Bow had outrun him. The seventh race was claimed by each. No one saw them run, so no one could decide the game. And they started quarreling.

Louder and louder their voices were raised. More and more angry they grew.

White Fawn, their mother, was baking corn bread on the coals of the wigwam fire. The angry voices reached her ears. She stepped to the door.

"For shame!" she called. "Go and set up your sticks."

Then she showed Lightning Bow and Flying Squirrel how to set up three sticks so they would stand for many days.

"Now go into the wood, set up your sticks, and leave your quarrel there," she said. "When the Berry Moon has passed, you shall return and see if the sticks are still standing.

"If they lean toward the rising sun, Lightning Bow was right. If they lean toward the setting sun, Flying Squirrel won. If they have fallen down, neither was right and neither won."

Lightning Bow and Flying Squirrel went into the wood and set up their sticks. Then they began to throw balls with willow wands, and soon they were happy again.

The sun had risen and set many times. The Berry Moon had passed. It was the Thunder Moon, when White Fawn said to Lightning Bow and Flying Squirrel, "Today you may go into the wood and see if your sticks are still standing."

Hand in hand, the two little Indian boys ran into the wood. They found only a heap of rotting sticks.

Flying Squirrel and Lightning Bow stood and looked at the sticks. They thought and thought.

"What did we set up the sticks for?" each asked of the other.

And for the life of them they could not remember what they had quarreled about, and why they had set up the sticks!

How the Mice Overcame the Warriors

Once, a tribe of the Iroquois became very warlike and cruel. They liked to follow the warpath rather than the hunting trails.

These warriors thought only of the war dance. They forgot to give thanks for the sweet waters of the maple, and for the planting season. Neither did they remember to praise the Great Spirit, in song and dance, for the juicy strawberries, and the waving green corn, as once they had done.

To fight was the one desire of their lives, the one thought that filled their minds. They boasted that none were so fierce and bloodthirsty as they.

"Our arrows fall like leaves of the pine," they said, "and always they are red with blood. Our war shirts have many scalp locks on them."

One day, a dispute arose with a neighboring tribe of their nation. The Peace Wigwam was not far away, but these warriors would not take their quarrel to it, as was the custom. The fighting Indians would have none of the Peace Wigwam.

"Let the women and papooses sit in the sun at the door of the Peace Wigwam," they said scornfully. "Chiefs are for the warpath."

A fierce cry was raised, and the war dance was begun. The chiefs painted their bodies, donned their war shirts, sharpened their  tomahawks, tipped their arrows, and tightened their bowstrings.

But by the time they were ready, the sun had set, and the blanket of darkness had fallen upon them. A council was quickly called. It was decided that they would not start to war until moonrise. So the warriors lay down to sleep.

As they slept, another council was called. This was not a council of men, but of mice.

From long and short trails they came, hundreds and hundreds of mice, for all had heard the warriors boast of their strength.

"Now," said the mice, "we will show these boasters how weak are men, and how strong are little mice."

When all the mice were gathered about the council tree, the leader spoke thus: "My brothers, listen! The Great Spirit did not give men strength, that they should fight and kill one another. The Great Spirit did not make men powerful, that they should strike down and kill the weaker animals. Let us show these fierce warriors that it is the weak who are strong, and the strong who are weak. Let every mouse destroy at least one weapon before the moon shall rise."

At this, all the mice set to work. Snap, snap, snap, went the bowstrings on all sides. Then the sharp little teeth began on the feathers that winged the poisoned arrows. Soon the feathers lay in bits about the ground.

Next, the deerskin cords that bound the sling shots were cut in two, and before the moon had risen, every weapon had been made useless. Every Indian had been disarmed—and the mice had scampered away.

The warriors awoke. Again the war cry was raised. They sprang to their feet and seized their weapons, but found them useless. Their bows had no strings; their arrows, no wings; their slings, no cords.

The warriors who boasted that they were the strongest and fiercest on the earth, had been made powerless by mice.

Why Crows are Poor

After the Great Spirit had made the Indians and had given them this beautiful land in which to live, he sent them a great gift—the gift of the corn.

Ga gaah, the Crow, claims it was he who brought this gift. He says he was called to the wigwam of the Great Spirit in the sky. A grain of corn was placed in his ear, and he was told to carry it to earth, to the Indians.

Therefore, as *Ga gaah* brought the gift, he claims he has a right to pull what corn he needs. *Ga gaah* says he does not "steal" corn. He simply takes what belongs to him, his rightful share.

And surely *Ga gaah* is not greedy! He never takes more corn than he wants for himself. He never hides or stores it away. He takes just what he wishes to eat at the time, and no more, for crows never think of tomorrow.

In summer, they are happy in the cornfields, guarding the roots from insect enemies, and pulling the tender blades whenever they are hungry.

But when winter comes, the crows are sad. Many councils are held. Sometimes a council tree will be black with crows. All are so poor and so hungry that they get together to try to plan a better way to live.

There is much noise and confusion at a crow council, for all the crows talk at once. All are saying, "No bird is so poor as the crow. He is always hungry. Next summer, let us plant and raise a big crop of corn, and gather and save it for the winter. Next winter, crows will not be hungry. We will no longer take from the fields of the Indians just enough corn for a meal today. We will raise our own corn, and keep a store for the winter."

And having agreed that this is a wise plan, the council ends.

A few days later, another council will be called. At this, the crows will plan how and where to plant the corn. Some will be appointed to select a field, others to find seed, and still others to plant and tend the corn.

But, alas! When spring comes, and skies are blue, and the sun shines warm, the crows forget the hunger of the winter, and the councils in the tree. They remember only that the skies are blue, and the sun shines warm, and now there is plenty of corn.

Happy and content, they walk up and down the fields of the Indians.

"We have all we want today," they say, "Why should we think of tomorrow, or next winter? We had a good meal this morning, and we are sure of one tonight. Is not this enough for a crow? What more can he ask?"

And the next winter comes, and finds the crows as poor and as hungry as they were the last. Again they are holding noisy councils in the council tree. Again they are laying plans for the great crop of corn that they will raise next summer!

Why the Indian Loves His Dog

The dog is the Indian's best friend. He is the comrade by day and the protector by night. As long as the Indian's dog has strength, he will fight for his friend.

The Indian says this is how the dog came to take his part.

An Indian and his dogs went into the woods to hunt. It was in the days when dogs and men could talk together, and each understood the language of the other.

When they reached the woods, the dogs began to talk with the Indian. They told him many wonderful things about the woods, which he did not know. They taught him many tricks of the chase: how to scent and track the game, and where to look for trails.

The man listened to what the dogs said, and he did as they told him. Soon the sledge which the dogs had drawn to the woods was piled high with deer and other game.

Never had the Indian's arrows brought him so much game. Never had he met with such success in hunting. He was so pleased that he said to the dogs, "Always shall I talk with you, give ear to what you say, and be one of you."

"Ah, but listen!" said the dogs. "If you wish to be one of us, you must live under the law of dogs, not men. Animals have laws different from those of men. When two dogs meet for the first time, they try their strength to see which is the better dog. Men do not fight when strangers meet, they shake hands. As we fight strange dogs, you too, must fight strange men, to see which is the best man—if you are to live under the law of dogs."

The man said he would think it over, and at sunrise give his answer. Indians always sleep before deciding a question.

Next morning, the man said he would live under the law of animals, and fight strange men.

The following day, the man made ready to leave the woods. From the basswood, he made a strong harness for the dogs, so that they could draw the load of game back to the camp for him.

When the sun was high, the man and the dogs started with the sledge load of game. They had not gone far before they saw two strange Indians coming.

"Now," said the dogs to the man, "remember you are living under the dogs' law. You must fight these strange men."

The man attacked first one Indian and then the other. At last both turned on him, and when they left him, he was nearly dead. At this, the dogs took a hand. They leaped upon the Indians and drove them from the woods. Then they came back to where their friend lay on the ground, and began to talk with him and lick his face.

The man could not speak for some time, but when his voice came to him, he said to the dogs, "No longer do I wish to live under the law of animals. No more shall I fight strangers. From this time, I shall shake hands with strangers, and bid them welcome. From this time, I shall be a man and live under the law of men."

"Then," said the dogs sadly, "we shall no longer be able to talk with you, and tell you the things that we know. But we will always stand by you. We will be your friends and will fight for you, when you need us as you did today."

This is why the Indian and his dog are now unable to speak each other's language. This is also why an Indian's dog will fight to the death for his friend.

Not only is the dog a true friend to the Indian in this world, but in the next as well. It seems that the soul of an Indian on its journey to the Happy Hunting Ground must cross a deep, swift-running stream. On either side of this dark river, there stand two dogs who hold in their teeth a great log upon which the souls pass.

The soul of the Indian who has been kind to his dog crosses the log easily, for the dogs stand guard. As the soul of such an Indian reaches the river, they say, "This Indian was kind to his dog. He gave him of his own food, and the dog always had a warm place by his fire. We will help this Indian to cross."

Then the dogs grip the log firmly in their teeth, and hold it steady while the soul of the kind Indian passes over.

But if the soul of an Indian who has been unkind to his dog comes to the river, the dogs say, "This man was cruel to his dog. He gave his dog no place by the fire, he beat him, he let him go hungry. This man shall not cross."

Then the dogs grip the log lightly in their teeth, and when the soul of the unkind Indian is half way across, they turn it quickly to one side, and the soul is thrown into the deep, dark river.

Many an Indian has been kind to his dog, so that he might make sure of a safe crossing on that log.

Greedy Fawn and the Porridge

In the days when there was no one living in this country but the Indians, there were no houses. There were only Indian wigwams. There were no roads and no streets, but Indian trails.

At that time there grew a wonderful chestnut, which the Indians used in their cooking. A very small bit of this chestnut grated into a kettle would make a potful of porridge.

In a certain wigwam lived Deerheart and Sky Elk, and their little son Greedy Fawn. The mother was called Deerheart because she was so loving, and gentle, and kind. The father was named Sky Elk because he was so strong and fleet of foot. Greedy Fawn, too, came rightly by his name. You will soon know why.

One day, Deerheart and Sky Elk went on a long trail. As they left the wigwam, they said to Greedy Fawn, "Do not touch the chestnut and do not build a fire while we are away."

Greedy Fawn promised. He watched his father and mother disappear down the western trail. Then he went back to the wigwam.

"Now," he thought, "I will have all the porridge I want."

So he ran and gathered some sticks. He built a fire with the sticks. Then he hung the kettle over the fire, and put some water in it. Then he found the chestnut. He grated a little of the chestnut into the kettle, and began to stir. Then he grated some more, and some more, and some more.

Faster and faster Greedy Fawn stirred the boiling porridge, for it began to swell and fill the kettle.

Larger and larger it grew, and grew, and grew.

Greedy Fawn was so frightened he did not know what to do.

"Oh, will it ever stop swelling?" he thought. Harder and harder he stirred to keep the porridge from boiling over. Beads of perspiration ran down his little bronze face, yet still he stirred. He dared not stop.

Then he remembered that sometimes his mother would tap the kettle with the porridge stick, if it became too full.

Tap, tap, tap, went the porridge stick on the edge of the kettle. Instantly the kettle began to swell. Larger, and larger, and larger it grew. Greedy Fawn was so frightened he did not know what to do.

Now Greedy Fawn could not reach across the kettle, to stir the porridge with his stick, so he began to run around it. And around, and around, and around the kettle he ran, stirring, and stirring, and stirring.

At last the kettle was so large that it nearly filled the wigwam. There was just enough space left for Greedy Fawn to run around it. And around, and around, and around the kettle he ran, stirring, and stirring, and stirring.

Oh, how his little arms ached! And, oh, how tired his small legs were! But still he ran. He dared not stop.

Here was porridge enough to last a small boy a lifetime, and he could not stop to taste one mouthful!

At last Greedy Fawn could run no longer. He stumbled and fell by the side of the kettle. He was too weak to rise. The stick fell from his hand, and the porridge boiled on. Higher, and higher, and higher it rose, until it ran over and down the sides of the kettle. Closer, and closer the boiling porridge crept to the little Indian boy, and soon Greedy Fawn and his stick were nearly buried in porridge.

For once, Greedy Fawn had all the porridge he wanted. And never again would he have wanted anything, had not Deerheart and Sky Elk heard his cries, and come running like deer up the trail to save him.

Why Hounds Outrun Other Animals

A hound was chasing a hare through the woods.

Some wolves and panthers were chasing a bull that had been feeding in the valley near the woods. For some time they had been trying to run him down, but they did not seem to gain on him.

When the wolves and panthers saw that they were not gaining on the bull, they halted to take counsel. They decided that it would take a whole day of hard running to get the bull, and a hound was near! Why not go for the hound?

All agreed. They set off for the hound.

Now the bull had heard the wolves and panthers take council, and he too, set off for the woods.

As he neared the wood, the bull called to the hound and warned him that a pack of wolves and panthers was after him. Just then they came into sight. The hound dared not meet them alone, and he knew not which way to turn.

Then the bull called, "Come, jump on my back. I can outrun them."

The hound ran and leaped on the back of the bull, and away they went.

The bull and the hound talked as they ran. The bull said he thought the wolves would soon grow tired, fall back, and give up the chase. But he was wrong. They were too angry at being outwitted.

"You think to take our game from us," they howled at the bull. "But we will eat hound meat tonight."

The bull saw it was a run for life. All day he ran. For a time it was easy to outrun the wolves and panthers, but at last they began to press hard upon him.

As the sun dropped out of the sky, the bull felt his knees begin to weaken. The weight of the hound was telling on him. A moment later, he stumbled and fell.

In an instant, the pack was upon them. But with one leap, the hound cleared the pack and was off down the trail.

The weaker wolves and panthers leaped upon the bull. The stronger went on.

But now the best of them were no match for the hound. He was fresh and strong, for he had been riding all day. They were tired and worn from the long chase, and soon they gave it up.

Because the hound is able to save his strength for the end of the chase, he can now outrun not only wolves and panthers, but all the other animals.

Why Indians Never Shoot Pigeons

An Indian hunter went into the forest in search of game.

The forest was so large that it would have taken three days to journey through it. All day he followed the track of the deer, but his arrows brought him no food.

At night, he came to a dark, swift-running stream. He was tired and hungry.

"Here," he said, "I will lie down and rest until sunrise."

He began to search for a bed of pine needles, for the Indian loves the pine tree. It is his friend by day and by night. By day it is his forest guide. At night it gives him a soft, sweet-smelling bed on which to sleep, and it shields him from the storm.

The hunter ran along the stream. It was very dark. He felt no soft pine needles under his moccasined feet, only the knotted roots of trees.

Suddenly the great roots of an oak tree reached out and caught him. He could not free his foot from the oak's grasp.

The sun rose and set. The great tree tightly held the hunter. He was weak from pain and hunger.

It was now two days since he had tasted food. Four notches had been cut in his stick, for the Indian measures time in this way. Each sunrise and sunset, when he is on the trail, is marked by a notch on a small stick which he carries.

Three times did the sun again rise and set, yet the tree did not let go of its hold. There were now ten notches on the stick, and the hunter was so weak that he could scarcely cut the last one.

As the sun rose on the fifth day, a bird flew into the tree. He saw the hunter lying on the ground, and came close and spoke to him.

The hunter understood, for in those days men and birds could talk together.

The bird asked the man what he could do for him, and the hunter whispered, "You are strong. You can fly a long trail. Go and tell the chief of my people."

The bird flew swiftly away with the message. He did not wait until the sun was high. He did not stop to eat one berry or one worm. He did not fly high, nor fly low to talk with other birds. He went straight to the people the hunter had told him of.

The West Wind tried to blow him back. A black cloud came up to frighten him, but he went through it. On, and on, and on, he went. Straight to the wigwam of the chief, he carried his message.

The chief had called together the young men who were fleet of foot, and was about to send them forth to find the lost hunter. They were asking the chief what trails they had best take. Before the chief could reply, a beautiful dove-colored bird had flown close to his ear and had spoken to him in soft, low tones.

The chief told the young men what the bird had said, and they set off on the trail the bird had named. Before sunset, they had found the lost hunter.

Carefully they freed him from the grasp of the great oak and brought him back to his people. That night there was a feast and a dance in his honor.

Ever since, the Indians have loved the birds that carry the messages, and they never shoot a pigeon.

How Old Man Winter Was Driven Back

Far away in the North Sky lives Old Man Winter. Every year he leaves his wigwam in the sky and comes to earth.

At the foot of a mountain, he builds a lodge of ice and snow, which no human being, animal or bird can enter. There he lives for a time.

North Wind is the only friend of Old Man Winter. When he passes near Old Man Winter's lodge, he gives a loud shriek, and with his blustering breath he blows open the door and enters.

Near a fire which glows, but does not warm, North Wind finds a seat. There he and Old Man Winter sit and smoke, and lay their plans for the next snowstorm.

When the council is ended, North Wind departs, to drive up the snow and hail from the corners of the earth.

Old Man Winter also leaves his lodge. He stalks over the mountains and valleys of the Indians. The land becomes white with his breath. The rivers are stilled, and all the voices of the wood are hushed as he passes. A deep sleep falls upon every living thing.

No sound is heard in the forest but the rapping on the trees. Old Man Winter carries a great hammer, and he strikes the trees a blow as he passes. The colder it grows, the louder and more frequently he raps. The trees snap, and the Indian lodges crack with his blows.

One day, as Old Man Winter was stalking through a forest, he came upon a hunter's lodge. For days the snow had been falling. No track of deer or rabbit was to be seen, and the hunter and his little boy sat within, weak from hunger. They were also very cold, for the fire in the lodge burned low.

Old Man Winter laughed and shook his hammer in glee, as he drew near. Once, twice, three times, he rapped. The little boy within heard him, and rapped three times in reply—just as Old Man Winter had done.

At this, the hunter spoke. He told the boy that he must not mock a nature spirit, lest some harm should come to him. He might be captured and made to serve that spirit.

Now when Old Man Winter heard the mocking raps of the little boy within the lodge, he was very angry. He breathed fiercely upon the little lodge. It shrank and shivered at his touch like a living thing. He struck it several sharp blows with his hammer, and passed on.

The fire inside the lodge burned lower and lower. The hunter and his little son drew closer and watched the last flame flicker and die out.

As they sat by the ashes, numb with the cold, all of a sudden, warmth filled the lodge. The South Wind gently opened the door, and a young chieftain, with a face like the sun, entered. He saw the dying hunter and the boy, and he warmed them back to life. When they were stronger, he helped them to rekindle the fire. Then he told them to take a few dried blackberries that they had in the lodge, and boil them in water.

He said they must eat a portion of the blackberries, and throw the rest at Old Man Winter when he returned. This would frighten him away, for he was terribly afraid of blackberries.

Blackberries mean sunshine and summer heat. Old Man Winter cannot stay where they are. He never visits the earth at blackberry time.

The hunter and the little boy said they would do as they had been told. Soon the young chieftain left the lodge, with the South Wind.

Not many days later, Old Man Winter returned, and again came rapping at their lodge. But this time the hunter and the little boy were ready. They threw the blackberries at him, as they had been told, and he ran in fear to his ice lodge.

The South Wind and the young chieftain with a face like the sun were near. They followed close upon the Old Man's track. When he was again inside the ice lodge, the South Wind rapped gently at the door.

"Be gone!" said the Old Man. "No one but North Wind is welcome to my lodge."

Then the South Wind breathed soft and warm upon the door of the ice lodge, and it melted at their feet. The young chieftain passed in and sat down by the strange fire that had no heat. The South Wind stayed, and sang, soft and low.

The Old Man was very angry. He raged about the lodge and ordered the young chieftain with sunshine in his face and warmth in his breath to depart.

"I am great and powerful," said the Old Man. "When I touch the sky, the snow falls. When I speak, hunters hide in their lodges; animals crawl into their holes; and birds fly in fear. When my hand touches the earth, it grows cold and hard, and all life dies. Be gone! Or I will make an ice man or a snow man of you."

But the young chieftain didn't move. He only sat and smiled at the bluster of the Old Man.

Slowly he filled a pipe, and handed it to the Old Man, saying, "Here, smoke with me. It will give you strength to go to your lodge in the North Sky. It is time for you to depart. You are old, and tired, and worn. You and North Wind have had your day. The days to come belong to South Wind and to me.

"I, too, am powerful, and I am young! I do not fear you. When I touch the earth, it grows soft and warm. Every living thing stirs in its sleep—birds and bees, flowers and trees, animals and men. When I speak, the sleeping sun awakes. See! Already he begins to send down his arrows. Hasten that they do not find you, on the trail to the North Sky."

The Old Man trembled. His legs and arms grew weak. Icicles fell from his beard. Great tears rolled down his cheeks.

"Who are you?" he whispered, as he was melting at the young chieftain's feet.

"I am **Go hay**—the spring," answered the young chieftain. "All the earth is glad, when I come to drive you back to your lodge in the North Sky, for I bring sunshine, and love, and joy."

But the Old Man did not hear. He was far on the North Sky trail, and Spring and South Wind were masters of earth.

Why Lightning Sometimes Strikes

An old man of the Iroquois nation once wished to make a beautiful Indian maiden his wife. The old man had many rare furs and valued strings of wampum. These he brought and laid at the door of the wigwam where the maiden lived.

 strings of wampum

The father and mother were pleased with the old man's gifts. They told him that when the Planting Moon should come, the maiden should go to his wigwam.

Now the maiden did not love the old man. She did not wish him to make her his wife. "I will never sit at his wigwam door," she said.

It was midwinter, when the old man brought the gifts, the time of the pale, cold moon. From that time, the maiden watched, with a heavy heart, the moons wax and wane.

At last the snows disappeared. No more was the North Wind heard shrieking about the lodge. The gentle South Wind had come, bringing with him the singing birds.

The little brooks awoke and sang. They were happy that spring had come, and all the earth children were glad—except the maiden. Her heart grew more heavy and sad, as the face of the sun grew brighter.

Then the Planting Moon came. The maiden watched the moon hang her horn in the sky. Then she ran swiftly to the great river that flowed not far from the lodge. Lightly she sprang into her canoe. A few quick strokes and the canoe was in midstream.

The current ran swift and strong. The little craft was carried swiftly down the river toward the great falls known as Niagara Falls. As the canoe neared the falls, the maiden was seen to rise and stretch out her arms, as though about to leap. A smile was on her face, and a song was on her lips, as the canoe shot into the mist that overhung the water.

Then, from the caverns below a dark blanket floated upward, as though spread to catch the maiden. It was Heno, the Thunder Spirit, who lived behind the falls. He had caught her in the folds of his blanket, and had saved her from the great rocks below.

Heno took the maiden to live with him, in his lodge behind the falls. There she was very happy, so happy that her smile shone through the mist, and the Indians cried, "See! A rainbow!"

In her new home the maiden learned many wonderful things. She found she possessed strange powers, not known to her before. She could float on a cloud at will, and she seemed filled with a strange fire.

One day, the young woman was given a son. Heno and she were very happy. Many moons the mother and child played together. When Heno was away on one of his journeys through the sky, they would ride the great bubbles of foam that went dashing through the rocks. Sometimes they would catch sunbeams in a net, as they sat on the edge of a cloud and fished.

One day, Heno asked the young woman if she would like to visit her people.

"If you wish," he said, "you shall return for a time, taking our son with you. But remember, both of you possess powers unknown to the earth children. Be careful how you use them. Never let another child strike the boy, for that child would at once wither and die. Never strike the boy yourself, for he would fall stunned to earth."

The woman listened to Heno's words. Soon they were wrapped in his great cloud blanket, and were floating over the river. When they came to the home of her people, Heno left the woman and the boy by the river, and went on further to the east.

The people were glad to see the woman, whom they had mourned as dead. She told them of the wonderful things she had learned in her new home. She told them also how Heno was freeing their land of a monster serpent that trailed underneath the earth, poisoning their springs and causing sickness. Always, she said, Heno carried a basket of great rocks on his back, which he hurled at the monster whenever he saw him. Soon he would kill the serpent, and they would be sick no more.

During many days, the mother and the little boy stayed with the earth people. Sometimes, when the child was playing by the river, he would see a dark cloud approaching. Then he would clap his hands with joy and cry, "There comes my father!"

The black cloud would float earthward, and Heno would stop and have a word with the mother and the boy. As he left them he always said, "Do not let anyone strike the boy."

But one day, the mother did not watch the boy, and he fell to playing with some earth children. They grew angry as they played, and struck the boy. Instantly these earth children fell dead to the ground. Then the mother laid hands on the boy, to punish him, and he fell to earth.

At this, there came a great rumbling and roaring through the sky, and Heno appeared. He took the lifeless child in his arms, crying, "You have disobeyed. No longer shall you have this great power I gave you. You shall remain on earth and be simply an earth woman. I will take the boy to my abode. Henceforth, our lodge shall be in the sky. There he will return to life, and ever after he will go with me on my journeys through the sky."

Then the sky shook and trembled. The door of the sky lodge opened, and Heno and the boy were seen no more.

Now, when a rumbling and rolling through the sky is heard, the Indians say, "'Tis the voice of Heno! He is coming from his lodge in the sky!"

Why the Hare has a Split Lip and a Short Tail

Once a rabbit began to run back and forth through the woods, calling for snow, snow, snow! It was one of those large gray rabbits with long ears that people call hares.

As this hare ran back and forth through the woods, he sang at the top of his voice, "***Ah gon ne yah—yeh! Ah gon ne yah-yeh! Ah gon ne yah—yeh! Dah gen, dah ton, Ah gon ne yah—yeh! Ah gon ne yah—yeh!***" This meant, "Snow, snow, snow! How I would run if I had snow! Snow, snow, snow! How I would run if I had snow!"

Now, strange as it may seem, as this hare ran back and forth singing for snow, snow, snow, some flakes of snow began to fall. The hare was so delighted that he jumped up and down for joy.

"***Ah gon ne yah—yeh! Ah gon ne yah—yeh! Ah gon ne yah—yeh!***" he sang, in short, quick notes of joy. And the higher he jumped, and the louder he sang, the faster and thicker the snow came.

The hare was so delighted that he again began to run. All day long he ran, back and forth through the woods, calling for "Snow, snow, snow! How I would run if I had snow!" And the snow fell faster and faster. Thicker and thicker it came. The path in which the rabbit ran grew higher and higher, as the snow fell deeper and deeper.

But at last the hare was so tired that he could run no longer. He no longer sang for "Snow, snow, snow! How I would run if I had snow," for now he had more snow than he wanted. The snow was up to the tiptops of the trees, and it was very hard to run.

The hare was very tired. He thought he must take a rest. Night was coming. He looked about him. Near the path were the top branches of a willow tree, sticking out above the snow. He sprang into a crotch of those branches. There he could sit and rest for a time. Soon he fell asleep. He slept all night and part of the next day.

That night it began to rain, and it rained very, very hard. The snow began to melt, and it melted very, very fast. When that hare awoke, not a flake of snow was to be seen!

But there was the hare away up in the tiptop of that willow tree! He did not know what to do. He was very hungry. He wondered how long he could stay there and not starve. He saw some tender buds on the branches. He ate those, and then he gnawed bark for a time.

However, sooner or later, the hare knew he must jump or starve. He looked down at the earth. It looked very good to him. He could see some fresh green moss and some beautiful grass. One jump, and they were his! But what a jump!

At last the hare whipped up his courage to the jumping point. He shut his eyes, and gave one great jump to earth. But when he jumped, he caught his tail on the branch of the willow tree and left part of it up there. And when he jumped, he struck the front of his face on a sharp stone, and the stone split his upper lip in two.

Ever since then, hares have had split lips and short tails, and ever since then, willow trees have had tails, or catkins, on them, in the spring.

Corn Plume and Bean Maiden

The Great Spirit had smiled upon his children. The land was filled with plenty, for the Great Spirit had given to them the three sustainers of life—the corn, the bean, and the squash. Flowers bloomed, birds sang, and all the earth was glad with the Indians, for the gifts of the Great Spirit.

On one side of a hill grew the tall, waving corn, with its silk tassels and plumes. On another side, beans, with their velvety pods, climbed toward the sky. Some distance down a third slope, beautiful yellow squashes turned their faces to the sun.

One day, the Spirit of the corn grew restless. There came a rustling through the waving leaves, and a great sigh burst from the heart of the tall stalks. The Spirit of the corn was lonely.

After that, every morning at sunrise, a handsome young chief was seen to come and stand on the brow of the hill. On his head were shining red plumes. Tall, and strong, and splendid he stood, wrapped in the folds of his waving blanket, whose fringed tassels danced to the summer breeze.

"**Che che hen! Che che hen**! Someone I would marry! Someone I would marry!" the young chieftain would sing, many, many times.

One day, his voice reached the Squash Maiden, on the other side of the hill. The Squash Maiden drew about her a rich green blanket, into which she had woven many flaunting gold trumpet-shaped flowers. Then she ran swiftly to the young chieftain.

"Marry me! Marry me!" said the Squash Maiden, as she spread her beautiful gold and green blanket at his feet.

Corn Plume looked down at the Squash Maiden sitting on her blanket at his feet. She was good to look upon, and yet Corn Plume was not content. He wanted a maiden who would stand by his side, not always sit at his feet.

84

Then Corn Plume spoke thus to the Squash Maiden.

"Corn Plume cannot marry Squash Maiden. She is very beautiful, but she will not make song in Corn Plume's heart. Squash Maiden will grow tired of his lodge. She will not stay in his wigwam. She likes to go on a long trail, and wander far from the lodge.

"Corn Plume cannot make Squash Maiden his wife, for he is not content with her. But she shall be Corn Plume's sister, and sit in his lodge whenever she will. The maiden Corn Plume weds must be ever at his side. She must go where he goes, stay where he stays."

Next morning at sunrise, the voice of Corn Plume was again heard, singing from the hilltop, "**Che che hen! Che che hen**! Someone I would marry! Someone I would marry! **Che che hen**! **Che che hen**!"

This time his song reached the ears of the Bean Maiden. Her heart sang, when she heard the voice of Corn Plume, for she knew that he was calling her. So light of heart was Bean Maiden that she ran like a deer up the hillside. On and on, up and over the brow of the hill she climbed, till she reached the young chieftain's side.

Then Corn Plume turned and beheld the most beautiful maiden he had ever seen. Her eyes were deep and dark, like mountain pools. Her breath was sweet as the waters of the maple. She threw off her blanket of green, and purple, and white, and stretched her twining arms to him.

Corn Plume desired to keep Bean Maiden forever close to him. He bent his tall plumed head to her. Her arms wound round and round the young chieftain, and Corn Plume was content.

So closely were the arms of Corn Plume and the Bean Maiden entwined, so truly were they wed, that the Indians never attempted to separate them. Ever after, corn and beans were planted in the same hill, and often a squash seed was added.

Since the Great Spirit had placed the corn, the bean, and the squash together on a hill, the Indian said they should continue to live and grow and occupy a hill together.

The door of Corn Plume's lodge was ever open to the Squash Maiden, if she chose to enter. But seldom did she stay in his wigwam. More often, she was found running off on a long trail.

But Bean Maiden remained true to Corn Plume. Always she was found by his side. Never did she leave the lodge unless he went with her. Corn Plume's lodge was her lodge, and her trail was his trail.

And because the Spirits of the corn and the bean are as one, the Indians not only plant and grow them together, but cook and eat them together. "In life, they were one," they say, "We will not separate them in death."

And now, when a great rustling and sighing of the corn is heard in the White man's land, the Indians often say, "'Tis the Spirit of Corn Plume, crying for his lost Bean Maiden!"

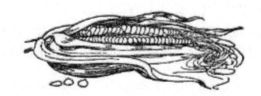

How the Robin Burned his Breast

Some Indian hunters once made their way north, to hunt for moose. It was at the time of Falling Leaves.

They journeyed for several days, until they came to a lake. Close by the lake they built a log cabin. Moss was placed between the logs to keep out the wind, and a thick roof was made from hemlock boughs. In the center of the roof, a small opening was left for the smoke from the lodge fire to pass out.

Here the hunters lived during the Moon of Falling Leaves. Every day they went on the moose trail, but they found no moose. Their arrows brought them little game of any kind. They became discouraged and sick, and one by one the hunters lay down and died.

At last there was but one hunter left. He, too, was sick, and he grew weaker day by day. His food was nearly gone. It was growing cold, and there was little wood in the cabin to burn.

But the man did not give up. Again and again he cried aloud, "Someone will come and help me! Someone will come and help me!"

One day, as he lay there too weak to rise, the fire flickered and went out. It seemed that he must die. But even then he did not give up. Again and again, with his weak voice he cried, "Someone will come and help me! Someone will come and help me!"

And someone did come and help him. His cry was heard when a bird came flying in through the smoke hole in the roof of the lodge.

The bird had such a cheery, brave voice that the man felt better the moment he flew in. The bird said to the man, "I was near and I heard you calling. I have come to help you."

Then the bird saw that the fire was out and that the man was cold. He fluttered among the ashes until he found a bit of live coal. With a glad chirp, he flew out through the roof. Soon he was back, with his bill full of dried twigs. He placed them on the fire and began to fan them into flame with his wings. Soon the twigs were blazing. Then he flew out for more twigs—and more, and more, and more.

The brave little bird kept on carrying twigs until the fire burned hot, and the lodge was warm once more.

When the bird had flown into the lodge, he had had a clean, white breast. After the fire was built, his breast was covered with red and brown spots. He tried to pick them off with his bill, but they would not come off. Instead, they seemed to spread, and his whole breast became red-brown. Then the bird knew that he must have burned his breast to a red-brown, when he was fanning the fire into flame.

But the little bird did not care if he had soiled his white breast, and burned it red-brown. Had he not brought cheer and life to a dying man?

He chirped a few glad notes then said to the man, "I will go now, but I shall be near your lodge. When you need me, call, and I will come again."

Later in the day, the man again called for help. The fire was getting low, and he was not yet strong enough to go out and gather twigs. Again the bird came to his aid. In and out he flew, many times, after small branches and twigs, until they were piled high on the fire, and once more it crackled and burned.

There was a little wood in the lodge. The man placed it on the fire, and the warmth healed the man, so that soon he was well and strong again.

Every day the man talked with the bird, for he was always near, and his cheery voice and brave words gave the man courage.

Once more he went on the moose trail, and this time his arrows brought him moose. In a short time the hunter had all the meat, skins, and moose hair he wanted. The moose hair he was taking to his wife, to work into pretty forms on moccasins.

The first snow was falling, as the hunter started south on the home trail. The bird hopped along by his side for a little way then said, "I must leave you now. Winter is coming, and I must be on my way to the

Southland, or the snow will catch me. In the spring you will see me again."

When spring came, the bird with the red-brown breast came with his mate, and built a nest close to the hunter's home lodge. In the nest, that summer, five little birds grew up, and they, too, had red and brown breasts.

And ever since, Robin Redbreast has continued to come and build his nest close to the lodges of men, for Robin Redbreast is a friend to man.

Iroquois Fairy Stories

How Morning Star Lost Her Fish

Once the Little People, the Indian fairies, ran with the Indians through the woods, and played with them beside the streams. Now they are not often seen, for the white man drove them out of the woods with the Indians, and away from the waters, with his big steam noises.

But before steamboats and great mills were on the streams, the Little People were there. They were often seen paddling their tiny canoes, or sliding down the great rocks on the banks. They loved to slide down a bank where one rock jutted out, for then they had a big bounce. They also liked to sport and jump with the fish.

There was a young Indian girl whose name was Morning Star. She was called Morning Star because her face was so bright, and she was always up early in the morning.

Morning Star lived with her father in a comfortable wigwam by a river. Every day she would get up with the sun, and run down to the river where the great rocks were, to catch fish for breakfast.

Morning Star caught her fish in a basket. At night, she would go and fasten her basket between the rocks, in a narrow place of the stream. Then, when the fish swam through in the night, they would get caught in it, and Morning Star would find plenty of fish waiting for her in the morning. Then she would take the basket of fish back to the wigwam, and soon the smell of fish frying on hot coals would come from the lodge.

Never since Morning Star began to fish with her basket, had Chief Little Wolf, her father, had to wait for his fish breakfast before starting on the chase. But one morning, neither Chief Little Wolf nor Morning Star breakfasted on fish.

This is how it happened.

On this morning, the Indian girl was up as usual with the sun. She ran down the river just as the Great Spirit lifted the sun's smiling face. Morning Star had such a light heart that she was glad just to be alive, and she sang a song of praise as she ran. All true Indians at sunrise lift their arms and faces to the sun, and thank the Great Spirit that he has smiled upon them again.

Happy and fleet as a deer, Morning Star ran on until she came to the great rocks. There she saw a whole tribe of tiny little folk gathered about her basket. Some of them were perched on the sides of the basket, laughing and singing. Others were lifting the fish from it and throwing them into the stream. Still others were opening and closing the splints of the basket for the fish to slip through.

Morning Star knew that these tiny folk were the **Jo gah oh**. She knew also that these Little People were friends of the fish. They know every twist of a fish net and every turn of a hook. Often they have been known to set fish free, and to guide them into deep, quiet places, far away from the men who fish.

Morning Star called to the Little People and begged them not to let all the fish go. Then she began to climb down the rocks, as fast as she could. The little Chief called up to her, "Fish, like Indian girls, like to be alive."

Then he told the Little People to keep on setting the fish free.

When Morning Star reached her basket, a few fish were still in it. She put out her hand to take them from the Little People—and not a fish or a **Jo gah oh** was to be seen. The Little People had darted into the rocks, for they go through anything, and the fish had slipped through the tiny spaces between the splints of the basket.

Morning Star heard the laughter of the Little People echo deep within the rocks, for they like to play pranks with the earth children. And far down the stream, she saw the fish leap with joy at being still alive. She took up her empty basket and went back to the wigwam.

That morning for breakfast, Morning Star baked corn cakes on the hot coals. As she ate the hot cakes, she thought they tasted almost as good as fish.

Ever after, when Morning Star saw a fish leap from the stream, she remembered what the **Jo gah oh** had said: "Fish, like Indian girls, like to be alive."

How Little Shooter Lost His Luck

One day, an Indian boy was playing beside a stream, when one of the little elf men came along in his canoe. The boy had his bow and arrow with him. So had the little elf man.

The little man stopped and offered to trade bows and arrows. The Indian boy looked first at his bow, and then at that of the little man. His bow was large. The little man's bow was very small. The boy thought his own bow was better, so he said he would not trade.

The little elf man laughed and drew his bow.

"You think only big things are great," he said. "Someday you will learn better. Someday you will want this little bow and these little arrows. Someday you will wish you had traded."

Then he shot an arrow into the clouds, sprang into his canoe, and paddled off up the stream. As he disappeared, he called back to the boy, "You will see me again sometime!"

The Indian boy ran to his wigwam home. He told his father about the little man he had seen, and how the man wanted to trade bow and arrows.

"And you did not trade?" exclaimed the father.

"No," said the boy, "his bow was small. Mine is large."

"Foolish boy!" said the father. "That little man was a **Jo gah oh**, one of the Little People. They do wonderful things. Their arrows are winged with power. Had you traded bows, you would have become a great hunter, and been able to get near the animals.

"Those little arrows of the **Jo gah oh** fly swift and far, and always bring back game. The boy who has a **Jo gah oh** bow and arrow always has good luck. One arrow of theirs is worth a flight of yours. Had you traded bow and arrows, you would have been called 'He shoots the sky.' Now you shall be called 'Little Shooter.'"

Little Shooter grew to be a man. He went often on the chase, but his arrows did not bring much game.

Many times, he wished he could meet the little elf man again, and trade bow and arrows, for sometimes he ran for days and found no track of deer or rabbit. But the little elf man never came.

One day, when Little Shooter had grown to be quite an old man, he was walking in the woods. He stopped under a tree to rest. Several times he felt something fall on his head.

At last he looked up to see what it was.

There sat the little elf man, swinging on the tip of a branch, and throwing nuts and twigs at him. He looked just as he did when Little Shooter met him by the stream long before. He had not grown old or changed at all.

"How long have you been here?" asked Little Shooter.

"I have always been here," said the little man. "I have been in the world ever since the stones were soft."

Then he laughed, and asked, "Does Little Shooter now like big bow and arrows best, or has he learned that sometimes small things are great? Next time, he had better trade with the little man," and aiming another nut at Little Shooter's head, he disappeared in the tree trunk.

How an Indian Boy Won His Name

It was bluebird time, many moons ago. Little brooks laughed and danced, and all the forest was glad.

An Indian boy came running through the forest. He, too, was glad, for it was spring!

As he ran down the trail, he saw something hanging from a bush. The bush was but a few rabbit jumps from the trail, so he stopped to see what new flower the spring had brought. He found the new flower to be a tiny papoose cradle.

The boy picked the cradle from the bush, and held it in the palm of his hand. As he looked closer, he saw that there was a tiny papoose in the little cradle. The wee papoose laughed in his face, as he spoke to it.

The boy had never seen so tiny a papoose, and he thought he would take it home to his mother. She had but nine of her own. He was sure she would like one more, and that there would be a place for the tiny stranger in their wigwam.

He started to run on down the trail, but something seemed to hold him fast. He could not get away. Three times he tried to run, but each time he only circled round that bush. Something held him to the spot.

Just then there came a sharp cry from up the trail. The boy thought some animal must be hurt or in pain. He turned to look and saw a little woman coming. She was less than a foot high, but she ran like a deer to the boy, and cried and begged him to give back her baby.

Then the boy knew it was the love of that little mother that had held him fast. He could not break the love cord between that mother and her baby.

Now the boy had a heart that was soft and kind. He liked to see everything happy. When he saw the little mother crying and begging for her baby, he felt sorry for her.

Many times he had heard his mother tell how every mother bird loves her young; every mother bear, her cub; every mother deer, her fawn; every Indian mother, her papoose. And he knew this little fairy mother must also love her fairy baby, so he put it on the little mother's back, and told her she should have her papoose.

The little mother gave a glad cry, as she felt the baby on her back once more. Then she drew a stone from a bag which she carried, and slipped it on a string of beads that hung from the boy's neck.

The stone shone on his breast like a dewdrop.

"Because you are good, and kind, and unselfish, and because you make everything happy," she said, "you shall wear this good-luck stone. It will bring you whatever you want. We Little People give this stone only to those earth children who are strong and yet protect the weak. Wear it always on your breast. Never take it off, and you will become a mighty chief."

Then the little mother gave another glad cry, and with her baby on her back she disappeared into an oak.

The boy ran on. His heart grew lighter and the stone brighter, as he ran. Before he reached his mother's wigwam, his arrows had brought back game for their evening meal.

From the day when the boy met the little **Jo gah oh** mother in the wood, and was given the stone, he had good luck. Whatever he did, all went well with him. If he went on the chase, he brought back deer. If he planted corn, it grew tall and fine. No boy could throw a ball as far, or could run as fast as he. He could shoot his arrows to the sky, and could send his snow-snakes skimming far beyond the rest.

So lucky was this Indian boy, that his tribe called him "Luck-in-all-moons."

"He wears the good-luck stone," the old people said as they sat around the fire, and they nodded their heads knowingly. But they never knew how he came by it, or why he won the stone.

And when "Luck-in-all-moons" grew to be a man, his tribe made him a great chief. Just as the little **Jo gah oh** mother had said, he became a chief, though not in the chieftain line.

Because he stood so strong and straight, serving the people, protecting the weak, and doing great deeds, he was called the Pine-tree Chief.

"His feet are planted deep in wisdom and strength," they said, "and his head is not far from the sky. He sees far and points us the way. As the topmost branch of the pine points always to the east, so Luck-in-all-moons shall guide us to the sun rising. He shall be our Pine-tree Chief."

How the Fairies Worked Magic

Once, a little Indian girl was very sad and unhappy. The Great Spirit had taken her father and mother, and she had gone to live with relatives who did not want her. Often she went to sleep hungry, for only the scraps of food that were left from a meal were given to her.

One day, the relatives of the little girl brought in a fine deer from the chase, and made ready for a feast. They told the girl to get out of the lodge, for there was neither room, nor meat for her.

The little girl ran and hid herself in a great field of corn. There she cried aloud.

Soon a band of strange Little People gathered about her, to comfort her. On all sides, from the folds of the green cornstalks they came.

They stroked her head, wiped the tears from her eyes, and said, "Don't cry, little girl. We will take care of you. You shall come and live with us. We will make a feast for you. We know why you are sad, for we can read the thoughts of all the earth children. Come with us, and we will show you more wonderful things than you have ever seen."

At this the little girl dried her tears, and smiled at the kind Little People.

"You are very good to me," she said. "Who are you?"

"We are the **Jo gah oh**," they replied, "the Little People. Come, and we will show you what we can do."

Then they slipped some winged moccasins upon her feet. They wrapped her in an invisible blanket and put a magic corn plume in her hair, and the next moment all were flying through the air.

They flew to a ledge of great rocks. At the touch of the Little People, the rocks opened, and they passed within.

The girl found herself in a beautiful lodge. Kind **Jo gah oh** mothers were baking cakes and roasting meat. They welcomed the girl, and soon a feast was spread in her honor.

Now the heart of the little girl was so light that she danced with joy.

"What wonderful people you are! Can you go anywhere, or do anything you wish?"

"Yes," said the little chief, "the **Jo gah oh** are small, but they are great. Come with us, and you shall see what we can do."

Again they were flying through the air. Soon they reached the lodge where the little girl had lived. It was night, and her relatives were asleep, but she could see the deer that hung outside ready for the feast.

"Now," said the **Jo gah oh** chief, "we will call out a pack of wolves from the wood yonder, and there will be no fat deer for this selfish feast, at sunrise."

Now no wolves had been seen in that wood for many moons. But at the call of the fairies, a pack sprang from it, ran to the lodge, seized the deer, and tore it into shreds. Then they again disappeared in the wood.

The little girl's eyes were large now with wonder, as they flew back to the fairy lodge in the rocks, but she was not afraid of these strange Little People. She was so happy with them she wished she might always live in a **Jo gah oh** lodge.

One morning, the little chief said, "Today we shall see more wonders."

This time a tiny canoe was waiting. They stepped into it and sailed down a river until they came to a great tree.

"In that tree," said the little chief, "lives a great, black bear. Every day he comes out that door you see high up in the bear tree. I will make the door fast so he cannot open it. A deep sleep will fall on him. He will sleep for many moons."

Then the chief threw three stones through the open door of the bear tree. Each time, a flame spread like a blanket over the door. A growling and scratching was heard within. Then all became still.

"Now," said the chief, "the bear will sleep until I call him in the spring. He is locked up for the winter. Come, let us go on."

The little girl drew her invisible blanket closer, as the canoe went sailing with the birds through the clouds. The birds that were swift of wing called loudly for a race.

"Come on!" said the fairy chief.

Then he spread wide the invisible sails of his canoe, and they flew past the birds like a streak of lightning. Even the eagle was left far behind. They seemed to shoot through the sky.

And, oh, what fun it was to be a bird! The little girl would have sailed on forever, but the little chief said, "You shall now return to your people. We have given them soft hearts and kind minds. They are calling for you. They will be glad to see you."

And soon the little girl was again in the wigwam of her relatives, sitting by the warm fire.

They greeted her with joy, spread a soft skin for her to sit upon, and gave her the best food. Ever after, the little girl lived with them and was happy.

Made in the USA
Las Vegas, NV
03 April 2023

70114421R00057